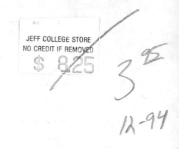

3 ^{E}

12-94

THE SATIRES OF
Juvenal

D0802558

The Satires of
JUVENAL

translated by Rolfe Humphries

Indiana University Press
BLOOMINGTON

Contents

Introduction

LITTLE IS accurately known about Decimus Junius Juvenalis, whom
we call Juvenal. Born at Aquinum, not so far from Monte Cassino, a
little later than the middle of the first century A.D., he spent much
of a fairly long and none too happy life in Rome, mostly during the
days of bad emperors, one of whom may have exiled him to Egypt,
whence he was recalled, maybe in late middle age, maybe a great
deal later. He may have been about sixty, he may have been eighty,
when he died. He took up writing in his maturity, not his youth; his
works seem to have made little impression on his contemporaries,
and to have burst on the world with excitement two and a half cen-
turies after his demise. The poet Martial addresses him (or some
one else with the same name) as a friend, but not as a fellow writer;

and Juvenal seems to have had no use for Pliny or any of his kin. The fact of which there seems to be least doubt is that he was a great writer of satire.

To Quintilian, and to Roman scholars and critics less well-known, the word *satire* had a meaning, and connotations, less narrow than it has for us. Into these, and into the history of the art form, we need not go, for satire, as Juvenal writes it, cries with the *saeva indignatio*, the slashing sense of outrage, that we associate with the term. He is Swift's cousin; we can feel at home. Not comfortably so, of course not, for this man is too good a hater.

What he hated were the ways of the world that Ovid, roughly a century before, had loved so dearly. *Beau monde, haut ton*—these did not amuse Juvenal. As for meretricious Rome, he shared the sentiments of (this too would have revolted him) an African king, Jugurtha the briber, dead before Ovid was born, who had called the city "venal and doomed if it only could find a purchaser." It had found, Juvenal thought, more purchasers than one, and more than one debaucher. He did not like it at all, and he said so.

That he had some warrant is attested by the roster of emperors under whom his days were spent. Nero, Galba, Otho (he is particularly scathing about Otho), Vitellius, Vespasian, Titus (these two were not so bad), Domitian, Nerva, Trajan, Hadrian. Domitian's fifteen years were a dreadful time; his successors were considerable of an improvement, and it may have been on his hopes of Hadrian that Juvenal founded the somewhat more optimistic addresses with which his seventh satire begins.

By Juvenal's day the status of the old middle class into which he was born had considerably worsened, degenerating from independence into cliency. In the good old days (which no satirist ever lived in) the relation between patron and client was an honorable one; not so now, with desperate avarice on one side and surly stinginess on the other. The decision of his friend Umbricius (Satire III) to abandon Rome for a little place near Cumae is the only decent way out; the city stinks with its native rabble and its sewage of foreigners, Greeks and Egyptians being the worst; the aristocrats, particularly their women, are noisomely corrupt; the higher the court, the baser its conduct. There are, to Juvenal's way of thinking, two egregious abominations around imperial thrones—the mincing favorites, the professional informers. See Satire II and Satire X for a bill of particulars. Some of this, even in our day, is not entirely untimely.

That Juvenal is fiercely angry there can be no doubt. What saves his work from the level of compulsive obsession (and it is sometimes a narrow escape) is, for one thing, his high-flying eloquence, the artful but grand quality of his rhetoric, the wild charge of his Rabelaisian humor. He is really quite funny sometimes. And, underlying this, and once in a rare while breaking through, is the lyrical tenderness which must be at the deep heart's core of every satirist, else how could he care so much? Parts of Satire III, for example: a scene near the beginning and the idyllic, almost Theocritan, close; a few lines of compassion over the briefness of life and the swift coming of old age, set in the rather repulsive detail of Satire IX; these bucolic verses from Satire XI—

"Now, Persicus, listen.
Here's what we're going to have, things we can't get in a market.
From a field I own near Tivoli—this you can count on—
The fattest kid in the flock, and the tenderest, one who has never
Learned about grass, nor dared to nibble the twigs of the willow,
With more milk in him than blood; and mountain asparagus gathered
By my foreman's wife, after she's finished her weaving.
Then there will be fresh eggs, great big ones, warm from the nest
With straw wisps stuck to the shells, and we'll cook the chickens that
    laid them.

9

We'll have grapes kept part of the year, but fresh as they were on the
    vines
Syrian bergamot pears, or the red ones from Segni in Latium;
In the same basket with these the lovely sweet-smelling apples
Better than those from Picenum. Don't worry, they're perfectly ripened,
Autumn's chill has matured their greenness, mellowed their juices."

The music here is not typical; in their usual run the hexameters of
Juvenal, almost as if they too were proving his argument about the
good old days, sound less like Ovid, Horace, Virgil, than they do
like Lucretius. There is something harsh and rugged about them;
they are not suave, but rough and tough and rugged. This is artistry,
not accident; what Juvenal is trying to do is to establish the importance of satire, to raise it above the offhand, the easygoing, to give it
not only mouth-filling sound, but epic stature. Do not mistake this,
he says in effect, for the critical but amiable lucubrations of a gentle-
man; kindly pay attention, I mean this, and the style is calculated to
prove it.

The Satires have not been translated into English verse in any
great profusion. Dryden rendered half a dozen of the sixteen, and
had various apprentices work on the others. Johnson's famous imi-
tation of the Tenth has fixed in our minds its title, On the Vanity of
Human Wishes. Gifford, in 1802, when Keats was seven years old,
brought out a version very much in the vein of the eighteenth century, showing no anticipatory stirrings of the peculiar sensitivity
that came in with the Romantics. All these translations, literal or
free, are in heroic couplets, a medium much more in the air, and in
the ears, of audiences from Dryden to Gifford inclusive than it is in
our own time. More's the pity, perhaps; but I am not entirely sure
that the polish, the linked-up wit, the fineness of this medium can
bring over to us Juvenal's rough, tough, slashing manner. I have ap-
proximated the original meter, dactylic hexameter. This meter, in

our usage, tends to gallop if not run away, Buckety, Buckety, Buckety, Buckety, Buckety, Bump down. We are not skilled at writing spondees; when we substitute for the dactyl it is as apt as not to come out with a miserable trochee. To keep Juvenal from sounding (*horresco referens!*) like Longfellow, or even like my own version of Ovid, *praeceptor amoris,* I have tried to be conscious of the dangers and to compensate by having my hexameters only roughly scannable, with here and there an iamb, just to be on the safe side. I do not guarantee that I have caught every single one of Juvenal's *double-entendres.*

My special thanks are due my colleague, Dr. Wendell Clausen, whose expert recension of the text of Juvenal will before too long be happily available to scholars. He has cast a charitable eye over the typescript and saved me at least a score of dubious renderings. I am also indebted to Professor Gilbert Highet for friendly notes and suggestions, and to Professor William Anderson, of Yale University, for his useful studies of Juvenal's patterns in structure.

ROLFE HUMPHRIES

Amherst, Mass.
May, 1958

THE LINE NUMBERS AT THE TOP OF EACH TEXT PAGE
ARE THOSE OF THE LATIN TEXT IN THE LOEB EDITION

THE SATIRES OF

Juvenal

On his compulsion
toward this form of writing

MUST I be listening always, and not pay them back? How they bore
    me,
Authors like Cordus the crude, with that epic he calls the Theseid!
What license have they for this, their endless ranting and droning?
Comedies, elegies—God! *Telephus* takes up a lifetime,
Orestes runs over the margins, whole volumes, and still never ends.

No man knows his own house any better than I know that grove
Where Mars dwells, or the cave under the Lipari Islands,
Vulcan's, that is. What the winds do there, or how Aeacus tortures
Ghosts in Hell, and who stole the Golden Fleece, and what ash trees

17

Monychus tosses around—all this is a noise and a shouting
Loud in the plane trees of Fronto, shaking the statues of marble,
Breaking the columns down with the din of inveterate readers.
You can expect the same themes from the greatest and least of the
    poets.
I submitted in school, and, slapped around on occasions,
Still gave Sulla advice to spend his days in retirement
Slumbering deep. I conclude, with doggerel bards all around us,
Sparing the page might be an act of mercy, but silly.

Still, if you have any time, or sense, or courtesy, let me
Tell you the reason why I urge my car on the drill ground
Where Lucilius drove the wheels of his chariot. Listen!
When a limp eunuch gets wived, and women, breasts Amazon-
    naked,
Face wild boars at the games, or a fellow who once was a barber
(I ought to know; he shaved me) grows richer than all the patricians,
When that spawn of the Nile, Curly the Cur of Canopus,
Hitches his crimson cloak with a jerk of his idiot shoulder,
Air-cools his summer ring, or tries to—his fingers are sweating—
And is unable to stand the burden of one more carat,
Then it is difficult NOT to write satire. What human being
Has such iron control of himself in this city of evil
As to hold his tongue, when he sees, for instance, the lawyer,
Matho, riding along in a new litter, bulging with Matho,
And at his heels his informer, the man who denounced his great
    friend,
The man who will soon enough snatch from the eaten-out nobles
Such as it is they have left, the terror of Lumpy the jester,
Greased by Dearie the dwarf with a bribe, with a lay by Miss
    Honey—

Why not? Her husband's afraid, and isn't she only an actress?
So you get jostled by earners (during the night shift) of heirlooms,
Raised to the heavenly heights by their service to some rich old bag:
Proculeius, one twelfth; Gillo, at least ten elevenths,
Each in proportion paid off to his due, the size of his tool.
Then let each, sure enough, take the price of his blood; let his pale-
    ness
Be like a man's who steps on a snake, barefoot; or a speaker's
Waiting his turn to orate in the competition at Lyons.
Why should I bother to say how my spleen burns dry with my anger
When, with his lackeys in droves, this ward cheater shoves folks
    around?
Here's another fine sort, found guilty—(the verdict is nonsense:
What does he care for the courts, just so he hangs on to his money?)
Marius, exiled, is drunk by noon; if the gods are offended,
That he enjoys; let the province weep in its impotent triumph!

Do not things like these rate the midnight oil of a Horace?
Should I not bring them to light? Why fool with those frivolous
    stories,
All about Diomed's horses, Hercules, and the Minotaur's bellow,
Icarus drowned in the sea, and Daedalus flying above him?
Why should I write about these, when a husband, both cuckold and
    pimp,
Takes from his wife's best friends monies the law won't allow her,
Perfectly trained, it seems, to keep his eyes on the ceiling
Or let his nose sound off as he goggles into his wine bowl?
Satire? What else, in an age when a youth can hope for a cohort,
Spending the family funds, to the last red cent, on the horses,
Dashing at breakneck speed, like the charioteer of Achilles,
Down the Flaminian Way, showing off to his top-coated girl friend?

How can you help but fill whole notebooks? Stand at the crossroads,
Here comes a forger of wills, all gotten up like Maecenas,
Borne along by six men in an exhibitionist's litter;
All it ever took to get him into the smart set
Was a paper scrap, and a seal too easily moistened.
Next comes some *grande dame*, who, when her husband is thirsty,
Puts toads' blood in his wine, and better than any Lucusta,
Shows less tutored girls how to cart off their husbands' black corpses,
What if the town does talk? If you want to be Somebody, these days,
Have the nerve to commit an act that rates jailing or exile:
Probity merits praise—and has to starve on the highways.
Crime pays off, in the form of gardens, palaces, tables,
Antique silver, with goats, standing out embossed, on the goblets.
How can you sleep, when some brides are males, and others, for
     money,
Cheat on a groom with his father, and teen-agers lay married
     women?
Talent perhaps I lack, but anger's an inspiration
Equally valid for me, and for poets like—Cluvienus!

I must cover it all in this olio, everything human,
Passion and prayer and fear, pleasure, distraction, and rage.
All the way back to the day when Deucalion went to the mountain
After the flood for his lots, and the stones grew softer and warmer,
All the way back to the day when Pyrrha showed the young men
Girls in their nakedness, and the rain clouds lifted and scattered,
When was there ever a time more rich in abundance of vices?
When did the jaws of greed ever open wider, or gambling
Have such consummate appeal? Men do not come to the tables
Only with wallets; they bring their safety-deposit boxes,
Epic occasions, these, with a secretary disbursing

Funds for the war. Is this, do you reckon, a simple madness,
Losing five thousand a throw, refusing a shivering slave
One thin shirt for his back? Which of our fathers erected
So many villas, or dined, alone, on seven-course dinners?
One little basket stands at the threshold; come get it, ye hungry,
Put your best clothes on! But first you must stand an inspection;
The patron must look at your face and be sure you are not an im-
    postor.
Advance to be recognized! He orders the herald to summon
Sons of the Trojan line; they crowd the portals, as we do.
"Give to the praetor first, and then to the tribune!" A freedman
Gets in the way. "I was first," he screams, "don't think you can scare
    me
Out of my place. Of course I was born on the banks of Euphrates,
That my earrings would prove, no matter how much I denied it.
Still, I own five smart shops that bring me in twenty thousand—
What senatorial stripe does any more for its owner?
Haven't I more than Licinus, or Pallas, or all of those fellows?
So get out of my way!" And so the tribunes stand waiting,
Wealth has the prior claim, and the badge of the sacred office
Counts for less than the chalk on the feet of the upstart invader.
Wealth, in our hearts, is set in the veriest Holy of Holies,
Though we have not yet built temples in honor of Money.
Oh, no! We worship Peace, Victory, Honor, and Virtue,
Harmony, too—and the storks clatter their bills in derision.

So, when the highest officials figure out, at the year's end,
What this dole brings in, how much it adds to their income,
What of the rank and file? This is their clothing, their footgear,
Bread on the table and fire in the stove. They come by the dozens,

Hands out for nickels and dimes, a man with his wife, sick or preg-
     nant;
Somebody else with a scheme—but the trick is all too familiar—
Points at a litter, closed, and claims a dependent's allowance:
"That's my wife inside. Hurry up, must we stand here forever?"
"Tell her to stick out her head!" "Aw, let her alone, she is resting."

So the day goes by with a lovely order of business:
First, this handout; then the forum, the courts of Apollo,
And the triumphal statues, including some lousy Egyptian's,
At the base of which only pissing's permitted.
There they go, the poor souls, old clients, weary and hopeless,
Though the last hope to leave is always that of a dinner,
They must buy cabbage now, and a little kindling to cook it.
Meanwhile, all by himself, on a couch unshared, their good king will
Gobble and guzzle the choicest products of land and ocean.
Down goes a whole estate; from such luxurious tables,
Broad and antique, down goes a whole estate at one sitting.
This will kill parasites off, at least; but who can endure this
Luxury, grudging and cheap? A whole roast boar for one gullet
When good custom decrees this is the fare for a party?
You will get yours pretty soon, when you go and undress in your
     bathroom,
Trying to ease your gut's distending burden of peacock.
Hence come sudden deaths, too sudden for old men to make wills.
What a good laugh for the town at all of the dinner tables!
Hear the disgruntled friends cheer at the funeral service!

To these ways of ours the future will add just nothing.
Our descendants' deeds and desires will follow the pattern.
Vice is at its peak. Set sail, O writer of Satire,

Spread your canvas wide. "But where," you may say, "is the talent
Worthy the theme, the passionate freedom of speech of our
    fathers?"
Who says now: "I dare name names, and if they don't like it,
What does it matter to me? Who cares about Mucius' forgiveness?"
Try that today, and what happens? You soon are a torch in a tunic
Standing where other men stand, victims, choking and smoking,
Till you fall, and your corpse makes a furrow across the arena.
What's that you say? "Must I accept the sneers of this fellow
Riding his cushioned ways, when I know he has poisoned three
    uncles?"
"Certainly. When he gets close, seal up your lip with your finger.
If you say, *Here he is*, some one will think you're informing.
You will be safe if you send Aeneas and Turnus to battle,
No one gets hurt if you write about the pride of Achilles,
Or how Hylas was sought when he fell in the well with his pitcher.
But when Lucilius roars and draws the sword in his anger,
Then the listener's mind, cold with its guilty knowledge,
Reddens and sweats; hence tears and wrath. You'd best think it over;
Once the helmet is on, it is much too late to be sorry."

All right, then. If I can't attack Tigellinus and his ilk,
Let's see what can be done about less fortunate mortals,
Those whose ashes lie by the great roads out of the city.

Against hypocritical queens

OFF TO Russia for me, or the Eskimos, hearing these fellows
Talk—what a nerve!—about morals, pretend that their virtue
Equals the Curian clan's, while they act like Bacchanal women.
Education they lack, though their parlors are crammed with bad
   statues,
Plaster casts of the Stoics, and each of them thinks he is perfect
If he has bought a bust of Aristotle, or maybe
One of the Seven Wise Men, or some disciple of Zeno's.
False fronts, all of them are. What street is not filled, overflowing
With these glum-looking queers? You rail at foul practices, do you,
When you're the ditch where they dig, the Socratic buggering per-
   verts?

Hairy parts, to be sure, and arms all covered with bristles
Promise a rough tough guy, but the pile doctor smiles; he knows
  better
Seeing that smooth behind, prepared for the operation.
They don't talk so much; their passion is rather for silence;
They keep their hair cut short, but oh, those wonderful eyebrows!
I like Peribomius better; at least he's honest about it,
Shows what he is by his walk and his glances, so I can excuse him,
Him and his likes, whose urge is frank enough for forgiveness.
Worse, much worse, are the ones who denounce, with a Hercules'
  anger,
Vice, and waggle their tongues about Virtue, and waggle their rear
  ends.
Sextus does things that Varillus observes and remarks, "How dis-
  gusting!"
Yet he does them himself. A white man can sneer at a Negro,
A cripple's a joke to the sound, but this is too much, that the Gracchi
Scream to high heaven against people they call rabble rousers.
This is confusion confounded, Verres denouncing a robber,
Milo opposed to assassins, Catiline chiding Cethegus,
Clodius damning adulterers, the second triumvirate shouting
Down with proscription! We had, and not long since, such a fellow
Who, in true tragic style, joined fornication with incest,
Then re-enacted the code which would horrify all human beings,
Not to say Venus and Mars, and while he was doing so, Julia
Rid her fertile womb of blobs that resembled her uncle.
Is it not perfectly right, therefore, that the vilest of sinners
Hate these hypocrites? If they snap at you, turn on them, bite them!

One of this sour-faced crew used to cry out, over and over,
"Where is the Julian law? asleep?" Laronia answered,

Smiling, "O happy age, with you to censor our morals!
Rome may be decent again with this Cato descended from Heaven,
But—tell me this, my friend: where do you purchase your perfume,
All that balsam juice your hairy neck fairly reeks of?
Don't be ashamed; let me know the address, the name of the drug-
　　gist.
Or if we have to rake up the laws and statutes, you ought to
Cite the Scantinian first, and the sections enjoining you fairies.
Go investigate men. They do more bad things than women.
Safety in numbers, you know, and your hollow squares will protect
　　you.
How you stick together, you queens! Our own sex's behavior
Holds no record like yours, case histories utterly loathsome.
Media doesn't lap girls, nor Flora go down on Catulla,
But Hispo takes on young men, and is pale from two occupations,
Do we ever plead at the bar? Does the courthouse ring with our
　　bawling?
Some of us do eat raw meat, and a few might be lady-wrestlers,
But look at you, spinning the wool, and mincing along with full
　　baskets,
Defter at weaving than ever Penelope was, or Arachne,
Doing the work that any cheap drab might squat on a log and ac-
　　complish.
Don't think I don't know why Hister bequeathed to his freedman
All he owned; why, in life, he rewarded his consort so richly.
She who sleeps third in a big wide bed is certain to prosper.
Marry, and shut your mouth; the wages of silence are jewels!
After all this, do you think our sex deserves a verdict of *Guilty?*
That's like pardoning crows and laying all blame on the pigeons."

That was telling them off, and they fluttered away, the fake Stoics,

27

Put to flight by the truth. Yet what won't they do? Here's a fellow,
Creticus, all dressed up in chiffon, while the populace marvels
Hearing his diatribes against the morals of women.
Fabulla, according to him, has broken the Seventh Commandment,
So has Carfinia; both, in his indictment, are guilty.
Guilty they both may be, but neither would put on a nightie
Thin as the robe he wears. "Oh, but," he says, "this weather—
These July days, my dear; but aren't they *frightful?* Just stifling!"
Strip completely, then; there's less disgrace if you're crazy.
Pretty garments indeed, to be seen with appeals and proposals
Made in the name of the law before the victorious people
Not yet healed of their wounds, or the hicks who've come down
    from the mountains,
Laying their ploughs aside, to open their mouths as they listen.
How you would shriek if the judge came out gowned in mosquito
    netting!
Have you any idea that a witness looks decent in gauze?
Creticus, you the keen, the intrepid apostle of freedom,
Wearing peek-a-boo clothes! But this disease is contagious,
It will infect more men, as the scab spreads all through the sheep-
    fold
From one sickly ram, as pig mange is epidemic
From one boar, or a rotten apple spoils the whole barrel.

No one hits bottom at once. Some day you will go a lot farther,
Dare something worse than this dress, and, little by little, be wel-
    comed
In the boudoirs where your friends run around with their foreheads
    in ribbons,
Earrings down to their necks, conducting, with sow tripes and wine
    bowl,

Services meant for the goddess who keeps men away from her
    threshold.
Only it's different here. "Remain far off, ye unholy!
Women, remain far off: no females play on our trumpets!"
So goes the cry, and the orgies blaze, like the torches, in secret.
Here's a lad making his eyebrows long, with damp soot on a needle,
Here's one taking a swig from a goblet shaped like a phallus,
Another one fixing his eyes, with a golden net on his long hair.
Here's one in sky-blue checks, another in pale-green satin
With a male maid who swears, as does the master, "By Juno!"
Another one holds a mirror, the scepter of Otho the Pathic,
Spoil of Auruncan Actor, wherein he saw himself armored,
Saw, and cried, *Off to the wars!* A remarkable piece of equipment,
Worthy of history's note, to be found in the gear of a soldier!
Such was the hero it took to knock off the doddering Galba
With no risk to his skin, or should we say, his complexion,
Masking his face with a mud pack of dough in his very last battle.
Who ever acted like this? Not Semiramis, bearing the quiver,
Not Cleopatra in gloom, on the deck of her Actian warship.
Here are no decent words, not even good table manners;
Here is freedom of speech, forsooth, in the piping falsetto
Cybele's priest affects, a crazy gray-headed old man,
Gobbler of any bird, a remarkable specimen, truly
Worthy his hire—but why don't they follow the Phrygian fashion,
Cut off the part they don't need? Why in the world are they waiting?

Gracchus has given a dowry, substance and sum, twenty thousand
To a cornetist, or maybe a type who plays the white flute.
Sealed, delivered, and signed. Happy Days. There's a crowd at the
    dinner.
The bride, almost in a swoon, reclines in the arms of her husband.

O ye nobles of Rome, is our need for a seer or a censor?
Would you be startled more, be more aghast at the portent
If a woman bore a calf, or a cow dropped a ewe lamb?
Here's an ancient house, long privileged, under tradition
To carry Mars' nodding shields along in the holy procession,
Sweating under their weight, the hands through the thongs of the
    leather,
Yet here's a son of that house, a Gracchus, given in marriage,
All tricked out in a veil, in a bridal train, and in flounces!
Romulus, father—whence came disgrace like this on your shep-
    herds?
Whence, father Mars, such an itch to fasten itself on your grand-
    sons?
Here is a man renowned for wealth, distinguished in breeding,
Being wed to a man, and you do nothing about it,
Not one shake of the helm, no spear point grounded in protest,
Never an outcry to Jove! To hell with you, father Gradivus—
Leave the neglected plains, the fields we used to call Martian.

"Early tomorrow," one says, "I have to go to a service—
Can you imagine?—at dawn." "What for?" "Oh, must you be ask-
    ing?
The marriage of one of my friends; only a few are invited."
Only a few! If we live long enough, they'll come out in the open,
Try to get their names in the paper's society pages.
Meanwhile, these dear little brides suffer one unspeakable torment:
They can't conceive, or give birth, and hold their husbands with
    offspring.
Well, that's all to the good, that nature denies to their bodies
What their appetites crave; no diet of hormones will help them.

No use to hold out their hands for Luperci to paddle with goat-
    thongs.
Sterile they die.
                But this vice is even outstripped by another.
Gracchus, dressed in a shirt, goes prancing around the arena,
Armed with the net, and ready to run if he misses. What baseness!
Gracchus, whose ancient line is prouder than that of Marcellus,
Catulus, Fabius, Paulus, the privileged class in the boxes—
Throw in the patron whose cash financed the show, for good meas-
    ure.
That there's a hell underground, and a dirty old god with a punt
    pole,
Croaking black frogs, and a skiff loaded with thousands on thou-
    sands,
Not even children believe, except those who are still in the nursery.
But suppose it were true—what would they think, the great heroes,
Curius, Scipios twain, the shades of the great-souled Camillus,
All the legion that fell at Cremera, the lost host of Cannae,
What would these high hearts feel when a prince like this came to
    join them?
Would they not cry out for sulphur and torches and laurel
Steaming with lustral smoke to bring them purification?

So, we have come to this. Our arms have invaded the Orkneys,
Ireland, the northern lands where the light dwells long in the sum-
    mer,
But the acts that are done in this proud city of victors
Never were done by the men we have beaten down. Wait! They
    tell us
Here's an Armenian prince, softer than all of our fairies,
Said to have given himself to some tribune's passionate ardor.

This, I suppose, could be called The Intercourse Between Nations.
An innocent hostage he came here, but Rome is where we make
    men.
Let them stay in our town, and lovers will never be lacking.
They can abandon their breeches, their bridles, their whips, and
    their daggers,
Bearing to Yerevan our Roman customs and culture.

Against the city of Rome

TROUBLED because my old friend is going, I still must commend him
For his decision to settle down in the ghost town of Cumae,
Giving the Sibyl one citizen more. That's the gateway to Baiae
There, a pleasant shore, a delightful retreat. I'd prefer
Even a barren rock in that bay to the brawl of Subura.
Where have we ever seen a place so dismal and lonely
We'd not be better off there, than afraid, as we are here, of fires,
Roofs caving in, and the thousand risks of this terrible city
Where the poets recite all through the dog days of August?

While they are loading his goods on one little four-wheeled wagon,
Here he waits, by the old archways which the aqueducts moisten.

33

This is where Numa, by night, came to visit his goddess.
That once holy grove, its sacred spring, and its temple,
Now are let out to the Jews, if they have some straw and a basket.
Every tree, these days, has to pay rent to the people.
Kick the Muses out; the forest is swarming with beggars.
So we go down to Egeria's vale, with its modern improvements.
How much more close the presence would be, were there lawns by
    the water,
Turf to the curve of the pool, not this unnatural marble!

Umbricius has much on his mind. "Since there's no place in the
    city,"
He says, "For an honest man, and no reward for his labors,
Since I have less today than yesterday, since by tomorrow
That will have dwindled still more, I have made my decision. I'm
    going
To the place where, I've heard, Daedalus put off his wings,
While my white hair is still new, my old age in the prime of its
    straightness,
While my fate spinner still has yarn on her spool, while I'm able
Still to support myself on two good legs, without crutches.
Rome, good-bye! Let the rest stay in the town if they want to,
Fellows like A, B, and C, who make black white at their pleasure,
Finding it easy to grab contracts for rivers and harbors,
Putting up temples, or cleaning out sewers, or hauling off corpses,
Or, if it comes to that, auctioning slaves in the market.
Once they used to be hornblowers, working the carneys;
Every wide place in the road knew their puffed-out cheeks and their
    squealing.
Now they give shows of their own. Thumbs up! Thumbs down! And
    the killers

Spare or slay, and then go back to concessions for private privies.
Nothing they won't take on. Why not?—since the kindness of Fortune
(Fortune is out for laughs) has exalted them out of the gutter.

"What should I do in Rome? I am no good at lying.
If a book's bad, I can't praise it, or go around ordering copies.
I don't know the stars; I can't hire out as assassin
When some young man wants his father knocked off for a price; I have never
Studied the guts of frogs, and plenty of others know better
How to convey to a bride the gifts of the first man she cheats with.
I am no lookout for thieves, so I cannot expect a commission
On some governor's staff. I'm a useless corpse, or a cripple.
Who has a pull these days, except your yes men and stooges
With blackmail in their hearts, yet smart enough to keep silent?
No honest man feels in debt to those he admits to his secrets,
But your Verres must love the man who can tattle on Verres
Any old time that he wants. Never let the gold of the Tagus,
Rolling under its shade, become so important, so precious
You have to lie awake, take bribes that you'll have to surrender,
Tossing in gloom, a threat to your mighty patron forever.

"Now let me speak of the race that our rich men dote on most fondly.
These I avoid like the plague, let's have no coyness about it.
Citizens, I can't stand a Greekized Rome. Yet what portion
Of the dregs of our town comes from Achaia only?
Into the Tiber pours the silt, the mud of Orontes,
Bringing its babble and brawl, its dissonant harps and its timbrels,
Bringing also the tarts who display their wares at the Circus.

35

Here's the place, if your taste is for hat-wearing whores, brightly
    colored!
What have they come to now, the simple souls from the country
Romulus used to know? They put on the *trechedipna*
(That might be called, in our tongue, their running-to-dinner out-
    fit),
Pin on their *niketeria* (medals), and smell *ceromatic*
(Attar of wrestler). They come, trooping from Samos and Tralles,
Andros, wherever that is, Azusa and Cucamonga,
Bound for the Esquiline or the hill we have named for the vineyard,
Termites, into great halls where they hope, some day, to be tyrants.
Desperate nerve, quick wit, as ready in speech as Isaeus,
Also a lot more long-winded. Look over there! See that fellow?
What do you take him for? He can be anybody he chooses,
Doctor of science or letters, a vet or a chiropractor,
Orator, painter, masseur, palmologist, tightrope walker.
If he is hungry enough, your little Greek stops at nothing.
Tell him to fly to the moon, and he runs right off for his space ship.
Who flew first? Some Moor, some Turk, some Croat, or some
    Slovene?
Not on your life, but a man from the very center of Athens.

"Should I not run away from these purple-wearing freeloaders?
Must I wait while they sign their names? Must their couches always
    be softer?
Stowaways, that's how they got here, in the plums and figs from
    Damascus.
I was here long before they were: my boyhood drank in the sky
Over the Aventine hill; I was nourished by Sabine olives.
Agh, what lackeys they are, what sycophants! See how they flatter
Some ignoramus's talk, or the looks of some horrible eyesore,

Saying some Ichabod Crane's long neck reminds them of muscles
Hercules strained when he lifted Antaeus aloft on his shoulders,
Praising some cackling voice that really sounds like a rooster's
When he's pecking a hen. We can praise the same objects that they
　　　do,
Only, they are believed. Does an actor do any better
Mimicking Thais, Alcestis, Doris without any clothes on?
It seems that a woman speaks, not a mask; the illusion is perfect
Down to the absence of bulge and the little cleft under the belly.
Yet they win no praise at home, for all of their talent.
Why?—Because Greece is a stage, and every Greek is an actor.
Laugh, and he splits his sides; weep, and his tears flow in torrents
Though he's not sad; if you ask for a little more fire in the winter
He will put on his big coat; if you say 'I'm hot,' he starts sweating.
We are not equals at all; he always has the advantage,
Able, by night or day, to assume, from another's expression,
This or that look, prepared to throw up his hands, to cheer loudly
If his friend gives a good loud belch or doesn't piss crooked,
Or if a gurgle comes from his golden cup when inverted
Straight up over his nose—a good deep swig, and no heeltaps!

"Furthermore, nothing is safe from his lust, neither matron nor
　　　virgin,
Not her affianced spouse, or the boy too young for the razor.
If he can't get at these, he would just as soon lay his friend's grand-
　　　ma.
(Anything, so he'll get in to knowing the family secrets!)
Since I'm discussing the Greeks, let's turn to their schools and pro-
　　　fessors,
The crimes of the hood and gown. Old Dr. Egnatius, informant,
Brought about the death of Barea, his friend and his pupil,

Born on that riverbank where the pinion of Pegasus landed.
No room here, none at all, for any respectable Roman
Where a Protogenes rules, or a Diphilus, or a Hermarchus,
Never sharing their friends—a racial characteristic!
Hands off! He puts a drop of his own, or his countryside's poison
Into his patron's ear, an ear which is only too willing
And I am kicked out of the house, and all my years of long service
Count for nothing. Nowhere does the loss of a client mean less.

"Let's not flatter ourselves. What's the use of our service?
What does a poor man gain by hurrying out in the nighttime,
All dressed up before dawn, when the praetor nags at his troopers
Bidding them hurry along to convey his respects to the ladies,
Barren, of course, like Albina, before any others can get there?
Sons of men freeborn give right of way to a rich man's
Slave; a crack, once or twice, at Calvina or Catiena
Costs an officer's pay, but if you like the face of some floozy
You hardly have money enough to make her climb down from her
    high chair.
Put on the stand, at Rome, a man with a record unblemished,
No more a perjurer than Numa was, or Metellus,
What will they question? His wealth, right away, and possibly, later,
(Only possibly, though) touch on his reputation.
'How many slaves does he feed? What's the extent of his acres?
How big are his platters? How many? What of his goblets and wine
    bowls?'
His word is as good as his bond—if he has enough bonds in his
    strongbox.
But a poor man's oath, even if sworn on all altars
All the way from here to the farthest Dodecanese island,
Has no standing in court. What has he to fear from the lightnings

Of the outraged gods? He has nothing to lose; they'll ignore him.

"If you're poor, you're a joke, on each and every occasion.
What a laugh, if your cloak is dirty or torn, if your toga
Seems a little bit soiled, if your shoe has a crack in the leather,
Or if more than one patch attests to more than one mending!
Poverty's greatest curse, much worse than the fact of it, is that
It makes men objects of mirth, ridiculed, humbled, embarrassed.
'Out of the front-row seats!' they cry when you're out of money,
Yield your place to the sons of some pimp, the spawn of some cat-
      house,
Some slick auctioneer's brat, or the louts some trainer has fathered
Or the well-groomed boys whose sire is a gladiator.
Such is the law of place, decreed by the nitwitted Otho:
All the best seats are reserved for the classes who have the most
      money.
Who can marry a girl if he has less money than she does?
What poor man is an heir, or can hope to be? Which of them ever
Rates a political job, even the meanest and lowest?
Long before now, all poor Roman descendants of Romans
Ought to have marched out of town in one determined migration.
Men do not easily rise whose poverty hinders their merit.
Here it is harder than anywhere else: the lodgings are hovels,
Rents out of sight; your slaves take plenty to fill up their bellies
While you make do with a snack. You're ashamed of your earthen-
      ware dishes—
Ah, but that wouldn't be true if you lived content in the country,
Wearing a dark-blue cape, and the hood thrown back on your
      shoulders.

"In a great part of this land of Italy, might as well face it,

No one puts on a toga unless he is dead. On festival days
Where the theater rises, cut from green turf, and with great pomp
Old familiar plays are staged again, and a baby,
Safe in his mother's lap, is scared of the grotesque mask,
There you see all dressed alike, the balcony and the front rows,
Even His Honor content with a tunic of simple white.
Here, beyond our means, we have to be smart, and too often
Get our effects with too much, an elaborate wardrobe, on credit!
This is a common vice; we must keep up with the neighbors,
Poor as we are. I tell you, everything here costs you something.
How much to give Cossus the time of day, or receive from Veiento
One quick glance, with his mouth buttoned up for fear he might
    greet you?
One shaves his beard, another cuts off the locks of his boy friend,
Offerings fill the house, but these, you find, you will pay for.
Put this in your pipe and smoke it—we have to pay tribute
Giving the slaves a bribe for the prospect of bribing their masters.

"Who, in Praeneste's cool, or the wooded Volsinian uplands,
Who, on Tivoli's heights, or a small town like Gabii, say,
Fears the collapse of his house? But Rome is supported on pipe-
    stems,
Matchsticks; it's cheaper, so, for the landlord to shore up his ruins,
Patch up the old cracked walls, and notify all the tenants
They can sleep secure, though the beams are in ruins above them.
No, the place to live is out there, where no cry of *Fire!*
Sounds the alarm of the night, with a neighbor yelling for water,
Moving his chattels and goods, and the whole third story is smoking.
This you'll never know: for if the ground floor is scared first,
You are the last to burn, up there where the eaves of the attic
Keep off the rain, and the doves are brooding over their nest eggs.

Codrus owned one bed, too small for a midget to sleep on,
Six little jugs he had, and a tankard adorning his sideboard,
Under whose marble (clay), a bust or a statue of Chiron,
Busted, lay on its side; an old locker held Greek books
Whose divinest lines were gnawed by the mice, those vandals.
Codrus had nothing, no doubt, and yet he succeeded, poor fellow,
Losing that nothing, his all. And this is the very last straw—
No one will help him out with a meal or lodging or shelter.
Stripped to the bone, begging for crusts, he still receives nothing.

"Yet if Asturicus' mansion burns down, what a frenzy of sorrow!
Mothers dishevel themselves, the leaders dress up in black,
Courts are adjourned. We groan at the fall of the city, we hate
The fire, and the fire still burns, and while it is burning,
Somebody rushes up to replace the loss of the marble,
Some one chips in toward a building fund, another gives statues,
Naked and shining white, some masterpiece of Euphranor
Or Polyclitus' chef d'œuvre; and here's a fellow with bronzes
Sacred to Asian gods. Books, chests, a bust of Minerva,
A bushel of silver coins. *To him that hath shall be given!*
This Persian, childless, of course, the richest man in the smart set,
Now has better things, and more, than before the disaster.
How can we help but think he started the fire on purpose?

"Tear yourself from the games, and get a place in the country!
One little Latian town, like Sora, say, or Frusino,
Offers a choice of homes, at a price you pay here, in one year,
Renting some hole in the wall. Nice houses, too, with a garden,
Springs bubbling up from the grass, no need for a windlass or bucket,
Plenty to water your flowers, if they need it, without any trouble.
Live there, fond of your hoe, an independent producer,

Willing and able to feed a hundred good vegetarians.
Isn't it something, to feel, wherever you are, how far off,
You are a monarch? At least, lord of a single lizard.

"Here in town the sick die from insomnia mostly.
Undigested food, on a stomach burning with ulcers,
Brings on listlessness, but who can sleep in a flophouse?
Who but the rich can afford sleep and a garden apartment?
That's the source of infection. The wheels creak by on the narrow
Streets of the wards, the drivers squabble and brawl when they're
    stopped,
More than enough to frustrate the drowsiest son of a sea cow.
When his business calls, the crowd makes way, as the rich man,
Carried high in his car, rides over them, reading or writing,
Even taking a snooze, perhaps, for the motion's composing.
Still, he gets where he wants before we do; for all of our hurry
Traffic gets in our way, in front, around and behind us.
Somebody gives me a shove with an elbow, or two-by-four scantling.
One clunks my head with a beam, another cracks down with a beer
    keg.
Mud is thick on my shins, I am trampled by somebody's big feet.
Now what?—a soldier grinds his hobnails into my toes.

"Don't you see the mob rushing along to the handout?
There are a hundred guests, each one with his kitchen servant.
Even Samson himself could hardly carry those burdens,
Pots and pans some poor little slave tries to keep on his head, while
    he hurries
Hoping to keep the fire alive by the wind of his running.
Tunics, new-darned, are ripped to shreds; there's the flash of a fir
    beam

Huge on some great dray, and another carries a pine tree,
Nodding above our heads and threatening death to the people.
What will be left of the mob, if that cart of Ligurian marble
Breaks its axle down and dumps its load on these swarms?
Who will identify limbs or bones? The poor man's cadaver,
Crushed, disappears like his breath. And meanwhile, at home, his
    household
Washes the dishes, and puffs up the fire, with all kinds of a clatter
Over the smeared flesh-scrapers, the flasks of oil, and the towels.
So the boys rush around, while their late master is sitting,
Newly come to the bank of the Styx, afraid of the filthy
Ferryman there, since he has no fare, not even a copper
In his dead mouth to pay for the ride through that muddy whirl-
    pool.

"Look at other things, the various dangers of nighttime.
How high it is to the cornice that breaks, and a chunk beats my
    brains out,
Or some slob heaves a jar, broken or cracked, from a window.
Bang! It comes down with a crash and proves its weight on the side-
    walk.
You are a thoughtless fool, unmindful of sudden disaster,
If you don't make your will before you go out to have dinner.
There are as many deaths in the night as there are open windows
Where you pass by; if you're wise, you will pray, in your wretched
    devotions,
People may be content with no more than emptying slop jars.

"There your hell-raising drunk, who has had the bad luck to kill no
    one,
Tosses in restless rage, like Achilles mourning Patroclus,

Turns from his face to his back, can't sleep, for only a fracas
Gives him the proper sedation. But any of these young hoodlums,
All steamed up on wine, watches his step when the crimson
Cloak goes by, a lord, with a long, long line of attendants,
Torches and brazen lamps, warning him, *Keep your distance!*
Me, however, whose torch is the moon, or the feeblest candle
Fed by a sputtering wick, he absolutely despises.
Here is how it all starts, the fight, if you think it is fighting
When he throws all the punches, and all I do is absorb them.
He stops. He tells me to stop. I stop. I have to obey him.
What can you do when he's mad and bigger and stronger than you
    are?
'Where do you come from?' he cries, 'you wino, you bean-bloated
    bastard?
Off what shoemaker's dish have you fed on chopped leeks and boiled
    lamb-lip?
What? No answer? Speak up, or take a swift kick in the rear.
Tell me where you hang out—in some praying-house with the Jew-
    boys?'
If you try to talk back, or sneak away without speaking,
All the same thing: you're assaulted, and then put under a bail bond
For committing assault. This is a poor man's freedom.
Beaten, cut up by fists, he begs and implores his assailant,
Please, for a chance to go home with a few teeth left in his mouth.

"This is not all you must fear. Shut up your house or your store,
Bolts and padlocks and bars will never keep out all the burglars,
Or a holdup man will do you in with a switch blade.
If the guards are strong over Pontine marshes and pinewoods
Near Volturno, the scum of the swamps and the filth of the forest
Swirl into Rome, the great sewer, their sanctuary, their haven.

Furnaces blast and anvils groan with the chains we are forging:
What other use have we for iron and steel? There is danger
We will have little left for hoes and mattocks and ploughshares.
Happy the men of old, those primitive generations
Under the tribunes and kings, when Rome had only one jailhouse!

"There is more I could say, I could give you more of my reasons,
But the sun slants down, my oxen seem to be calling,
My man with the whip is impatient, I must be on my way.
So long! Don't forget me. Whenever you come to Aquino
Seeking relief from Rome, send for me. I'll come over
From my bay to your hills, hiking along in my thick boots
Toward your chilly fields. What's more, I promise to listen
If your satirical verse esteems me worthy the honor."

Against a big fish

CURLY the Cur again! I shall have to summon him often
Onto our stage, this monster, with not a redeeming virtue,
Vicious, debauched, and sick, but strong in adulterous passion,
So much so that he scorns widows and unmarried women.
What difference does it make that his colonnades are extensive,
Tiring his horses and mules, that he rides in the shade of his wood-
     lands,
That he's bought acres adjoining the forum, and God knows what
     mansions?
No bad man is well-off, least of all a seducer, whose incest
Gets him to bed with a Vestal, a virgin who must, in atonement,
Lie under earth while her blood still runs alive in her veins.

Now to more trivial acts. And yet, if another had done them,
John Doe or Richard Roe, he would run afoul of the censors.
What's disgraceful for them is quite all right for our Curly.
What are we going to do? His person is even more loathsome
Than any charge we can bring. He paid off for a mullet, a red one,
Three hundred bucks. That comes out to fifty dollars a pound.
Shrewdness like that I'd praise, and call it the work of an artist,
If such expense insured his name in an old man's will,
Or—this would make more sense—if he spent it on some great fe-
     male,
Who scorns the public gaze, in her litter with outsize windows.
No such thing; he bought this for himself. Remember the gourmet,
What was his name? Apicius? Curly makes him look cheap,
Curly, who used to run around in a jock strap of paper,
Pays for a mullet this much. The silly fish must have cost him
More than the fisherman would. You could buy an estate in a prov-
     ince
At that price, or less (it would partly depend on the dust storms).
What kind of feasts should we think His Imperial Majesty gobbles,
When one purple punk of the Palatine pukes up all this,
One side dish, so to speak, from his rich and opulent banquet?
Curly, head man in the court, is the same one who used to go bawl-
     ing,
Peddling shad, broken lots, in the Alexandrian alleys!

O Muse of Epic, begin! Will the audience kindly be seated?
No fictive music now, but the facts. Relate them, ye Pierian maid-
     ens!
(Calling you maidens, I hope, will serve me to some advantage.)

When the last of the Flavian line was flaying the world, half-lifeless,

And Rome was the slave of a Nero, the bald-headed tyrant Domi-
tian,
Lo, a remarkable thing befell. Off Doric Ancona,
Where the temple of Venus towers high on the headland,
Into the nets there fell a leviathan of a turbot,
Huger than those that lie under the ice of Maeotis
Till it is cracked by the sun, and its denizens, sluggish and torpid
From the long cold, thaw out, disembogued at the Black Sea har-
bors.
This huge fish the owner of boat and tackle has saved up
For the Great High Priest—for who would dare put on the market,
Who would dare buy, such a fish, with the shores alive with inform-
ers?
Every inspector of seaweed would pounce like a hawk on the cap-
tain,
Ready to swear and depose, and with many a witness to back him,
That the fish had been fed in His Majesty's ponds, had absconded,
Must, as a fugitive, be duly returned to The Master,
Citing authorities like Armillatus and Sura,
Who prove that everything handsome and rare that swims in the
ocean,
Ipso facto, belongs to the royal kitchen. So, give it
Rather than let it spoil.
              The deadly season of autumn
Yields to the frost; sick men begin to hope for their seizures
Every fourth day, not third. The ugly winter is whistling
With his refrigerant breath to keep the booty from spoiling.
Here comes a man in a rush, as if afraid of a south wind.
Below him lie the lakes where Alba, although in ruins,
Still keeps the Trojan fire and worships Vesta the lesser.
There, for a while, his progress is blocked by the awe-struck traffic.

49

Then it gives way, and the doors, on easy hinges, swing open.
The fish goes in. Shut out, the gentlemen of the Senate
Stand there and stare. Inside, in His Majesty's Awful Presence,
The man from Picenum speaks: "Receive," says he, "an oblation
Too great for a private kitchen. Be this a day of thanksgiving,
Purge Thy royal gut of the last full feast it has eaten;
Gorge on this turbot, saved for Thy gracious administration.
He insisted on being caught." What could be cruder? And yet
The great man beams in pride. There is nothing he cannot give
     credence
When it's about himself, when his power is praised equal to Heav-
     en's.
But there's no dish big enough for the fish!
                                        Summon the council,
Men whom the emperor hates, men on whose blanching faces
Sits the sign of that great and most uncomfortable friendship.
"Hurry!" the chamberlain calls, "Our Royal Master is seated!"
Pegasus dashes in first, grabbing his gown in his hurry,
Overseer, newly set up in charge of a city bewildered.
What could officials be but overseers in those days?
This was one of the best, a devout and scrupulous jurist,
Even in evil times tempering justice with mercy.
Crispus came next, a pleasant old man, whose manner of speaking
Proved his gentle soul. At the side of an absolute monarch
Who might have been of more use, if he were only permitted,
Under that pest, that plague, to raise his voice, to condemn
Savage counsels of hate, to express his honest opinions?
Nothing more prone to caprice than the sensitive ear of a tyrant
On whose whim depends the fate of a friend, who is safest
Talking about the heat, or the rain, or the clouds in the springtime.
Crispus never flailed his arms upstream in that current,

Crispus wasn't the man for freedom of speech and the spirit,
Betting his life on the truth. So, Crispus lived many winters,
Saw his eightieth year, safe, in that court, by such armor.

Next to him hurried a man his age; his name was Acilius.
With him came his son, a decent youth, whom an ill death
Waited for, not much later, sped by the swords of his master.
A miracle, in our time, to reach old age and be noble!
Better not get too big: a little brother to giants,
That's high enough to aspire. It availed young Acilius nothing,
Fighting naked with lions and boars in the Alban arena.
Who, in our time, does not see through the wily tricks of patricians?
Who would wonder today at the simple cunning of Brutus?
When our kings wore long beards, it was easy enough to deceive
    them.

Rubrius, looking no better, came next. He wasn't a noble.
That may have been reassuring, but then, he had been convicted
Of an old offense, and one that is better not mentioned,
Worse than the sodomite Nero, who lashed other pathics with satire.
Montanus was there. He was late because of the size of his belly.
Curly the Cur was there, who reeks, in the morning, with odors
That would outstink the smell of at least two funeral parlors.
Pompey was there, an informer whose whisper could cut your throat,
Fuscus, whose battles were planned in hallways of Parian marble,
Tactics just the right sort to suit the vultures of Poland.
Careful Veiento came, and with him the deadly Catullus
Burning with love for a girl he had never seen. What a portent,
Even for times like these! He was blind, but a flattering fawner,
Sinister, one who belonged with the beggars infesting the bridges,
Swarming out to the wheels, or blowing the richer ones kisses.

No one was more amazed at the fish than he was; he gestured
Toward the left as he spoke; it happened to be on his right.
That was always his way, if he praised some Cilician bruiser
Or the stage machines that lift the boys to the awnings.
Veiento was almost as bad; carried away by his frenzy
Almost into a trance, he presently vaticinated:
"Omens of triumph I see, my Lord. Thou wilt capture a monarch
Foreign-born like this turbot, Arviragus of the Britons.
This I can tell by the spiky fins erect on the backbone."
Fabricius went on and on; the only thing he omitted
Was the place where the fish spawned and the actual date of its
    birthday.

"What think you? cut it up?"—"My Lord," Montanus says, "Never!
Spare it such mortal disgrace, but let a deep shell be provided
Ample to hold in its delicate sides these giant dimensions.
What such a dish needs now, at once, is fire-bringer Prometheus!
Hurry with clay and wheel! But from henceforward, Great Caesar,
Let potters follow your camp!"
                              The motion was duly carried,
Worthy, it seemed, of the man who knew the debauches of Nero's
Midnight hunger and thirst, his lungs inflamed from the wine cups.
No man, in my day, was a more experienced eater.
He could tell, with one bite, where an oyster was born, where it
    came from,
Whether the Lucrine Rocks, or the beds of Richborough, England.
Just one glance, and he'd tell you any sea-urchin's home port.

Meeting adjourned, council dismissed. They are ordered to get out,
Men whom this mighty Lord had dragged posthaste to this castle,
Frightened, in panic, expecting news of invasions by Germans,

Desperate tidings borne from every part of the empire.
Would that to nonsense like this he had given all his devotion,
Spared that savage caprice which took away from the city
Bright illustrious souls. No retribution, no vengeance!
Nobles he could kill. He was soaked in their blood, and no matter.
But when the common herd began to dread him, he perished.

Against mean patrons, and despicable clients

TREBIUS, if you persist in these ways, so utterly shameless
That you think it is the highest good to live on another man's table,
If you can stand for treatment the cheapest satellites never
Would have endured at the unjust board of an earlier Caesar,
Then I'd not trust your word under oath. I know, it takes little,
Little enough, to keep a belly content; if that's lacking,
Is there no place on the sidewalk, no room on one of the bridges,
No smaller half of a beggar's mat where you could be standing?
Is a free meal worth its cost in insult, your hunger
So demanding? By God, it would be more honest to shiver
No matter where you are, and gnaw on mouldy dog-biscuit.

First, get this into your head: an invitation to dinner
Means a payment in full for all of your previous service.
One meal is your share of the profit of this great friendship. Your master
Puts it on your account, a rare enough entry, sufficient,
Just the same, to balance his books. Perhaps two months later
It may please him again to invite his neglected client
Lest the lowest place at the lowest table be empty.
"Join us," he says. The height of good luck! What more could you ask for?
Trebius has good cause to break off his sleep, to come running,
Shoelaces not yet tied, worried that some one else,
Or every one else, may arrive before he does with his greetings,
While the stars fade out in the early hours of the morning,
While the planets wheel, sluggish and cold in the heavens.

What a dinner it is! Blotting paper would shudder
To sop up wine like this, which turns the guests into madmen.
"You bastard!" "You son of a bitch!" These are preliminaries
To the main event, a battle royal, the freedmen
Versus the rest of you, with goblets and crockery flying.
You stop a jug with your face, pick up a napkin to wipe it,
Find your bloody nose has turned the damask to crimson,
While your host drinks wine drawn off when the consuls were bearded,
Juice of grapes that were trod during wars a hundred years past.
Will he send one thimbleful to his cardiac friend? No. Never.
Tomorrow he'll drink again, a vintage from Setian or Alban
Mountains, the jar so black with soot and dust that he cannot
Tell where it came from, what year, such wine as Paetus and Priscus,

Chaplet-crowned haters of Tyrants, would drink on republican
    birthdays
Honoring Brutus and Cassius.
                              Your noble patron, this Virro,
Holds cups encrusted with amber, saucers jagged with beryl,
Never letting them go; to you no gold is entrusted,
Or, if it ever is, a watcher leans over your shoulder
Keeping count of each jewel, watching your sharpened nails.
Pardon precautions like these, but his jasper is wonderful, truly.
Virro, and many like him, transfer from their rings to their goblets
Stones like these, the kind Aeneas wore on his scabbard.
You will drink from a cup that is cracked and fit for the junk pile,
Tradable, maybe, for sulphur, one of those four-nozzled vessels
Named after Nero's fool, the cobbler Beneventum.

If his stomach's inflamed from the food and wine, he is given
Water, sterilized first by boiling, then cooled in the snow.
You did not get the same wine, I complained; that's half of the story,
The water is different, too. You are handed the cup by the fellow
Who runs in front of his car, a Gaetulian out of the stables,
Or by the bony hand of some black Moor, not a person
You'd enjoy meeting at night where the tombs line the roads of the
    city.
Standing in front of your host is the very flower of Asia,
Bought for a higher price than the whole estates of old kings,
Tullus, the fighter, and Ancus, were worth. In fact, you could throw
    in
All of the goods of all of the kings of the Rome of the legends.
This being so, if you thirst, look for your African server.
His expensive boy cannot mix a drink for a poor man,
But he's so lovely, so young! When do you think he will listen,

Whether it's hot or cold you request? Oh no, it's beneath him
To serve an old client; he's irked that you ask, or sit while he's
    standing.
Every great house is full of these supercilious slave boys.
Look at this one, who grumbles, handing you the hard bread
Made of the coarsest bran, or the mouldy jawbreaking crackers.
But our lord receives the tenderest, snowiest, finest
Proof of the kneader's art. Respect the breadbasket, please!
Keep hands off! If you reach—such nerve is hard to imagine—
Some one will cry, "Put it down! You shameless guest, can't you ever
Learn which kind is yours, and tell your bread by its color?"
Was it for this, you'll think, that you left your wife in the morning,
Ran up hill through the cold, with the hail rattling down in the
    springtime,
With your porous cloak distilling water in buckets?

In comes a lobster, immense, in fact, too large for the platter,
Waving its tail in contempt at the crowd, as it rides along, high-
    borne,
To the table's head, with asparagus for a garnish.
What do you get? One prawn, half an egg—the kind of a supper
People leave at the tombs of the dead by way of a token.
He soaks his fish in the best olive oil; you get some pale coleslaw
Reeking of stuff that would smell very fine if used in a lantern,
Grease that has ridden the Nile in the meanest African lighters.
Used as a lotion, it gives you absolute privacy, bathing,
Guaranteed, furthermore, as a preventive of snake bite.
Virro will have a mullet, from Corsica or Taormina,
Since our seas are fished out, so desperate are our gluttons.
Too many nets are spread near home, and our Tuscan fishes
Never attain full size, so the provinces have to supply them.

That's where the market is found by the legacy-hunters. Lacnas
Makes his purchases there, and Aurelia sells, at a profit.
Virro is given a lamprey, the greatest that Sicily ever
Sent to our coast; when the wind from the south is still in his prison,
Drying his wings, all craft despise the wrath of Charybdis.
You get an eel, so-called, but it looks much more like a blacksnake,
Or you may get a pike from the Tiber, mottled with ice-spots,
A riverbank denizen, fat from the rush of the sewers,
Tough enough to swim uptown as far as Subura.

A word in the ear of our host, if he'd be so kind as to listen:
"No one asks for such gifts as Seneca, Piso, or Cotta
Sent to their humble friends, when giving was reckoned an honor
Greater than titles or symbols of power. All we can ask for
Is that you dine with us on decent terms, just another
Citizen like ourselves. Do this—all right, all right, we can't stop you
Being rich for yourself and poor to your friends. They all do it."

What comes in now? Goose liver, tremendous, and also a capon
Big as a goose, and a boar, worthy of blond Meleager's
Steel, served piping hot, and truffles, assuming the season
Right for their growth, with enough spring thunder to swell their
    production.
What did that gourmet say? Alledius, I think his name was—
"Keep your wheat for yourself, O Libya; unyoke your oxen,
Just so you send us your truffles!"
                              Meanwhile, to make you more angry,
You will behold the carver, the sleight-of-hand master, performing,
Prancing around, and waving his knife like a wand. How impor-
    tant,
So his master says, to make the right gestures when carving

Rabbit or fowl! Shut your mouth, don't act like a freeborn Roman,
Don't think those three words of your name have any real meaning.
Do you want to be dragged from the house by the heels, like Cacus
 the monster
After the beating he took from Hercules? When will Virro
Pass you the cup? He won't. And he won't risk any pollution
Touching his lips to the rim which a wretch like you has infected.
Which of you has the nerve, is so abandoned or silly
As to say to that prince "Drink up!" When your jacket is shabby
There are many remarks it is better to leave unspoken,
But should a god, or some chap who looked like a god, be more
 kindly
Than your fates ever were, and give you the cool twenty thousand
Suiting the rank of knight, how quickly you'd find yourself Some
 One,
Not a nobody now, but Virro's most intimate crony.
"Something for Trebius there! Give Trebius one more helping!
Brother, wouldn't you like a cut from the loin?" Money, money,
You are the one he calls brother, the one he gives homage and
 honor.
One word of caution, though: if you want to be patron and prince,
Let no little Aeneas go playing about in your hallways,
Let no small princess appear as father's small sweetheart.
Nothing will bring you more friends than a wife who is certified
 barren,
But, the way things are now, should your wife present you with
 triplets,
Virro'd be utterly charmed with your chattering brood, and to show
 it,
Order for each a little green shirt, and peanuts, and pennies,
When the small parasites come and hang around at his table.

Toadstools the poor will get, but Virro is feasted on mushrooms
Such as Claudius ate, before the one his wife gave him.
(Since then, he ate no more.) To himself and the rest of the Virros
Fruit will be served. Such fruit you'd be happy with even a smell
    of,
Fruit such as grew in the days when Autumn was never-ending,
Fruit you would think had been robbed from the girls of the Golden
    Orchards.
You get a rotten old apple, the kind that is given a monkey
All rigged out with a helmet and shield, and afraid of a whipping
While he is being trained to toss the spear from a goat's back.

Maybe you think that Virro is cheap. That's hardly the reason.
He does this to hurt, on purpose. What comedy ever,
What buffoon, is more fun than a gut that rumbles in protest?
So, in case you don't know, all this is done to compel you,
Force you, to tears of rage, and the grinding of squeaky molars.
You're a free man (you think) and the guest of a royal good fellow.
He knows, too damn well, you're the slave of the smell of his
    kitchen.
Oh, he's perfectly right. Only a slave would endure him
More than once. I don't care how poor you were in your childhood,
Whether you wore on your neck amulets golden or leather.
You are sucked in, now, by the hope of a dinner. "He'll give us,
Surely," you say, "at least the remains of a rabbit, the scraps
Off a wild-boar's haunch, or a picked-over carcass of capon."
So you sit there dumb, all of you, silent, expectant,
Bread in your hand untouched, ready to spring into action.
He's a wise man to treat you like this, for if you can stand it,
You can stand anything else, and, by God, I think that you ought to!

Some day you'll offer your shaved-off heads to be slapped, and a
    flogging
Won't seem fearful at all. You have done what you could to deserve
    them,
Trebius. Such a feast! And such a wonderful friendship!

Against women

CHASTITY lingered on earth, I believe, in the reign of King Saturn.
She was seen then, for a while, a long time ago, when cold caves
Offered men tiny homes, and enclosed, in their common shadow,
Fire and the household god, the herd and the owner together.
Those were the days when a mountain wife had a mattress to lie on,
Made out of leaves or straw or the hides of the native creatures.
There were no city girls like Cynthia, known to Propertius,
None like the one who wept, red-eyed at the death of her sparrow.
No: these women had breasts for big fat babies to tug at.
Often they looked as rough as their acorn-belching husbands.
Men were different then, when the world and the skies were younger,
Sons of the riven oak, or scions of clay, unfathered.

Under Jove, it might be, you could still distinguish the footprints
Chastity might have left, but that was when Jove was a stripling,
Not yet the time when the Greeks swore oaths (and broke them); when no one
Feared the thief in his cabbage or fruits, when his garden was open.
Justice, by slow degrees, deserted earth for the heavens,
Chastity at her side, and so the sisters departed.

Postumus, it's an old custom, hallowed by ancient tradition,
To bounce another man's bed, put horns on the brow of its genius.
Every other crime came in the Era of Iron,
But the Silver Age, earlier still, first saw the rise of these cheaters.
Yet, in a time like ours, here you are, preparing for marriage,
Contracts, and pledges, and banns, and your hair getting combed by a barber
Un vrai maître de coiffure, and perhaps you have bought her the ring.
Surely you used to be sane. Postumus, are you taking a wife?
Tell me what Fury, what snakes, have driven you on to this madness?
Can you be under her thumb, while ropes are so cheap and so many,
When there are windows wide open and high enough to jump down from,
While the Aemilian bridge is practically in your back yard?
Or if no such way out appeals to you, isn't it better
To get some young boy in your bed to sleep with you in the night-time
Without threatening suits or insisting on costlier presents,
Uncomplaining if you refuse to breathe hard at his bidding?

But the Julian law suits you fine. So you want a sweet little youngster,
Heir to your vast estate, though you'll have to do without squab,

Filet of catfish, and all the nice legacy-bait of the market.
Postumus, what can't be done, if a woman takes you for a husband?
You, most notorious rake of all the tail-chasers of Rome,
You, who have hidden in closets, or under the bed of some cuckold,
You stick your silly head in the marital noose? You go seeking
A virtuous old-fashioned wife? It's time to summon the doctors.
What a real sweetheart you are! If a decent and modest woman
Falls to your lot, flop prone on your face at the Tarpeian altar,
Bow and adore, and slay a golden heifer to Juno.
Not many women are worthy to touch the fillets of Ceres,
Many the ones whose kisses even their fathers recoil from.
So hang wreaths on your door, adorn the lintel with ivy!
Will she be satisfied with one man, this piece of perfection?
Sooner, I think, with one eye. But you keep insisting you've heard of
One who lives at home on the farm, with a great reputation.
Well—let her live in some one-horse town as she lives in the coun-
  try,
Maybe I'll learn to believe in this wonderful rustic virtue,
But did you never hear about things that happen in mountains,
Happen in caves? Are Mars and Jupiter utterly senile?

Do you think our arcades can supply a woman worth your devotion?
Do the rows of our theatres hold one you can love without anguish,
One you could choose from those tiers? Tuccia wets her pants
Watching the soft Bathyllus dancing the ballet of Leda.
Appula sighs or cries as she does in the climax of passion.
Thymele watches both, the sudden comers and slow ones.
She's a country girl, but learning her country matters.
After the curtain goes down, and the theatres close, and the court-
  rooms
Offer the only show through the humdrum months of the summer,

Then the women, bored, go in for the mask and the thyrsus,
Not to say Accius' tights. Urbicus gets a big laugh
Taking off Autonoe; poor Aelia's crazy about him.
Some of these women pay high for a comic to loosen his codpiece,
Some like tragedians better, or stifle the voices of tenors.
What did you think they would do—go read the works of Quin-
        tilian?
You are taking a wife who will make Echion a father
(He plays the lyre); if not him, it might be the flute player, Am-
        brose.
Let's put up the long stands through the narrow streets of the
        city,
Drape the doorposts with laurel, happy in celebration
Over the birth of your noble son, who reveals, in his cradle,
Features much less like yours than the mug of some gladiator.

Eppia, wife of a senator, followed one of these gentry
Off to that town by the Nile, the Alexandrian cesspool,
But even that town condemned our monstrous manners and morals.
She had no thought of her home, her sister, husband, or country,
Wickedly left her children in tears, and—this will astound you!—
Even forsook the games and that marvelous Thespian, Paris.
Reared in luxury's lap, and pillowed on down of the softest,
She had no fear of the sea, and no fear for her reputation—
That's not much to lose, in the minds of cushion-bred ladies.
So, with a heart unafraid, she faced the roar of the oceans,
All of the swing of the seas. Consideration of danger,
If a woman is honest, chills her heart with foreboding,
She shakes at the knees, hardly can stand, so great is her terror.
But your bold ones have great nerve for their shameful adventure.
Tough, to embark on a ship, in case a husband requires it,

The sky keeps whirling around, and the smell of the bilge water's
    dreadful,
But if it's a lover she follows, her stomach is made of cast iron.
She would puke on her spouse, but now she feeds with the sailors,
Wanders all over the ship, has fun in hauling the hand ropes.

What was the youthful charm that Eppia found so enchanting?
What did she see worth while being labelled "The Gladiatress"?
This dear boy had begun to shave a long while ago, and one arm,
Wounded, gave hope of retirement; besides, he was frightfully ugly,
Scarred by his helmet, a wart on his nose, and his eyes always run-
    ning.
Gladiators, though, look better than any Adonis:
This is what she preferred to children, country, and sister,
This to her husband. The sword is what they dote on, these women.
Once discharged, he would seem of no more use than Veiento.

What do you care for the life of Eppia, and her adventures?
Look at those peers of the gods, and hear what Claudius suffered.
Soon as his august wife was sure that her husband was sleeping,
This imperial whore preferred, to a bed in the palace,
Some low mattress, put on the hood she wore in the nighttime,
Sneaked through the streets alone, or with only a single companion,
Hid her black hair in a blonde-colored wig, and entered a brothel.
Reek of old sheets, still warm—her cell was reserved for her, empty,
Held in the name of Lycisca. There she took off her dress,
Showed her golden tits, and the parts where Britannicus came from,
Took the customers on, with gestures more than inviting,
Asked and received her price and had a wonderful evening.
Then, when the pimp let the girls go home, she sadly departed
Last of them all to leave, still hot, with a woman's erection,

67

Tired by her men, but unsatisfied still, her cheeks all discolored,
Rank with the smell of the lamps, filthy, completely disgusting,
Perfumed with aroma of whore-house, and home, at last, to her
    pillow.

Why mention philters and spells and brews of virulent poison
Given a stepson? They do worse things, these lust-ridden women.
At the bidding of sex, the least of their sins are committed.

"But why does her husband swear Censennia's the noblest of wom-
    en?"
She brought him a million, that's why; for that he should call her
    chaste.
He is not faint from the arrows of love, nor burnt by those torches,
No—it's the dowry that brings the fire, that loosens the arrows.
Liberty at a price! She may beckon and write whom she pleases.
Rich wives of greedy husbands have all the license of widows.

"Why does Bibula fire Sertorius' passionate ardor?"
If you want the truth, it's the face he loves, not the wife.
Let three wrinkles appear, let her skin become flabby and dry,
Let her teeth turn black, or her eyes appear to grow smaller,
He, or his freedman, will tell her, "Pack up your bags and get going.
You are a bore and a pest, forever blowing your nose.
Out of the house and make room for a woman who isn't a snot-
    nose!"
Meanwhile, she's always on fire, a queen, who extracts of her hus-
    band
Shepherds, Camerian sheep, and elms for Falernian vineyards.
That's the least of it, though: she wants all of his houseboys, his
    work gangs.

If he doesn't have things his neighbor has, let him go out and buy
    them!
In the wintertime, when Jason the Trader is hidden,
When the booths at the fair hide the murals of sailors in armor,
Then she picks up huge vessels of crystal, huge jars full of myrrh,
Comes home wearing a ring, the diamond of Berenice,
Well-known in legend (which adds to the cost), the stone King
    Agrippa
Gave his incestuous sister in that barbarian country
Where, on the Sabbath day, the kings will go around barefoot,
Where the pigs are free to live to a ripe old age.

"Isn't there one from all of these crowds who seems to you worthy?"
Let her be well-behaved, good-looking, wealthy, and fertile,
Let her have ancestors' busts and portraits all over her hallways,
Let her be more intact than all the pre-ravished Sabines,
Let her be a rare bird, the rarest on earth, a black swan—
Who could endure a wife endowed with every perfection?
I would rather, much rather, have a Venusian girl
Than the noble Cornelia, mother of heroes, those Gracchi,
Bringing, with all her virtues, those upraised and haughty eyebrows,
Counting as part of her dowry parades and processions of triumph.
Spare me your Hannibals, please, and your Syphaxes, conquered in
    camp;
Get to hell out of here with your Carthage, whole kit and caboodle!

Remember Amphion's prayer: "Spare them Apollo, Diana!
The children are not to blame; aim the darts at the mother!"
But the bow twanged on, and Niobe followed her children,
Followed their sire, to the tomb. Why? Her inordinate pride
Made her seem, to herself, more noble because of her offspring

Than Latona was, or the Alban sow with her litter.
Are they worth so much, all the beauty, all the decorum
Thrown up to you all the time? Excessive pride of the spirit
Turns the honey to gall; there's simply no pleasure in it,
All that high and rare, that high and mighty perfection,
And is there any man such a prey to uxorious worship
That he does not dread the wife he extols to the heavens,
Does not hate her at least fourteen hours out of two dozen?

Even some trivial things are most offensive to husbands.
What stinks worse than the fact that none of them trust their good
    looks
Till they have made themselves Greeks and jabber away in that
    language?
(Though it's a bigger disgrace to speak ungrammatical Latin.)
All their gossip, their fears, their anger, their joys and their worries,
Their intimate secrets of soul, they pour out in Greek. I can tell you
They even go to bed in Greek with their *Zoe* and *Psyche*
My Life and *My Soul*. My word! This might be forgiven in school-
    girls,
But when you're eighty-six, such raptures are hardly becoming
Zoe and *Psyche—my life and my soul*: you're using in public
Words that are better kept for under the sheets in the bedroom,
Words whose effect and intent were better left to your fingers.
Croon in the smoothest tones that an Elvius ever might gurgle,
You will flutter no dovecotes; the lines in your face are too ancient.

If you're not going to love your lawfully wedded wife,
Why get married at all? Why waste the supper, the cookies
Given the guests, already stuffed to the ears, as the party breaks up?
Why waste the first night's gift of a golden tray, or a salver

Rich with inscriptions that tell of victories over the Germans?
If you are simply devoted to one alone, bend your neck,
Bow to the yoke; no lover finds mercy in any woman.
Passionate she may be, but she loves to plunder and torment.
The better you are, as husband and man, the less the advantage
You will get from a wife. You will never give anyone presents
If she says, *No!* If she stands in your way, there is nothing, but noth-
    ing,
You can purchase or sell. She will regulate even your friendships,
Slam the door in the face of a lifelong boon companion.
Gladiators and pimps and masseurs and similar gentry
Make their wills as they please, but no such luck in your household;
Your estate must be left to more than one of your rivals.

"Crucify that slave!" "But what has he done to deserve it?
Who is witness against him? Who has informed on him? Listen—
No delay's ever too long in the death of a human being."
"A slave is a human being? You fool! All right, he's done nothing.
This is my wish, my command; my desire is good enough reason."
So she is lord of her spouse. But soon she abandons this kingdom,
Occupies house after house, and her bridal veil gets pretty ragged,
Then she comes flying back to the bed she scorned and abandoned,
Leaving behind her the doors in festal array, and the garlands
New on the walls, and the branches still green over the lintel.
So her conquests grow: eight husbands in five Octobers—
O illustrious feat, worth being carved on her tombstone!

If your mother-in-law is alive, kiss concord farewell.
She eggs on the wife to rejoice in despoiling the husband
Stripped to the bone; she gives instructions in answering letters—
Nothing simple or crude now!—sent by her daughter's seducers.

She is the one who deceives the guards at your door, or else bribes
    them.
Your wife may be perfectly well, but she loves to call in the doctor,
Haul off the blankets—too heavy!—and meanwhile the lover, in
    hiding,
Silent, can hardly wait, and wonders how long he can stand it.
What do you think?—that a mother can give her daughter instruc-
    tion,
Teach her decent ways, when there's no decency in her?
Not a chance in the world. Like mother, like daughter. The old one
Knows where advantage lies, and bawdry profits from whoredom.

Almost no day in court goes by without cases which women
Prompt, one way or another, plaintiff, defendant, no matter.
They draw up the briefs themselves, prepare the indictments,
Ready to draft or dictate all of the speeches of counsel.

Who does not know of the blankets that women drape over their
    shoulders
After athletic workouts, the pastes they use for their rubdowns?
Who has not seen the dummies of wood they slash at and batter
Whether with swords or with spears, going through all the maneu-
    vers?
These are the girls who blast on the trumpets in honor of Flora.
Or, it may be, they have deeper designs, and are really preparing
For the arena itself. How can a woman be decent
Sticking her head in a helmet, denying the sex she was born with?
Manly feats they adore, but they wouldn't want to be men,
Poor weak things (they think), how little they really enjoy it!
What a great honor it is for a husband to see, at an auction
Where his wife's effects are up for sale, belts, shinguards,

Arm-protectors and plumes! Or a different kind of a skirmish,
Maybe, has taken her fancy, one where she won't need a girdle,
Won't want a thing on her legs, not even so much as a stocking.
These are the women who sweat in the thinnest, most flimsy of gar-
　　ments;
Even the sheerest silks are too hot for their delicate bodies.
Hear her grunt and groan as she works at it, parrying, thrusting;
See her neck bent down under the weight of her helmet;
Look at the rolls of bandage and tape, so her legs look like tree
　　trunks,
Then have a laugh for yourself, after the practice is over,
Armor and weapons put down, and she squats as she uses the vessel.
Ah, degenerate girls from the line of our praetors and consuls,
Tell us, whom have you seen got up in any such fashion,
Panting and sweating like this? No gladiator's wench,
No tough strip-tease broad would ever so much as attempt it.

The bed holds more than a bride; you lie with bicker and quarrel
Always, all night long, and sleep is the last thing you get there.
There she can really throw her weight around, like a tigress
Robbed of her young; or else, to atone for her own bad conscience,
She fakes the outraged sigh, and hates the boys whom her husband
Has, or she says he has, or sheds tears over a mistress
Purely fictitious, of course. Her tears come down like the raindrops,
With plenty more where they came from, ready to flow at her bid-
　　ding.
Abject slug that you are, you think this proves that she loves you.
Aren't you pleased with yourself, as your lips go seeking those lashes
Wet with her pitiful tears? But what if you happened to open
The drawers of her desk, and found those notes, those fervent epis-
　　tles,

Saved by your green-eyed wife, the hypocritical cheater?
You may catch her in bed with a slave or a knight. What happens?
All she can do in that case is invoke the art of Quintilian,
"Master of Rhetoric, help! Come to my aid, I implore you."
"Sorry," Quintilian replies, "I'm stuck; get yourself out of this one."
This does not bother her much; her explanation is ready.
"Long ago," she says, "it was understood between us
Perfectly well, you could do what you pleased, and no double stand-
    ard
Kept me from having my fun. So howl as much as you want to,
I am human, too." Can you beat their nerve when you catch them?
That's when their very guilt supplies them anger and spirit.

Where, you ask, do they come from, such monsters as these? In the
    old days
Latin women were chaste by dint of their lowly fortunes.
Toil and short hours for sleep kept cottages free from contagion,
Hands were hard from working the wool, and husbands were watch-
    ing,
Standing to arms at the Colline Gate, and the shadow of Hannibal's
    looming.
Now we suffer the evils of long peace. Luxury hatches
Terrors worse than the wars, avenging a world beaten down.
Every crime is here, and every lust, as they have been
Since the day, long since, when Roman poverty perished.
Over our seven hills, from that day on, they came pouring,
The rabble and rout of the East, Sybaris, Rhodes, Miletus,
Yes, and Tarentum too, garlanded, drunken, shameless.
Dirty money it was that first imported among us
Foreign vice and our times broke down with overindulgence.
Riches are flabby, soft. And what does Venus care for

74

When she is drunk? She can't tell one end of a thing from another,
Gulping big oysters down at midnight, making the unguents
Foam in the unmixed wine, and drinking out of a conch-horn
While the walls spin round, and the table starts in dancing,
And the glow of the lamps is blurred by double their number.

How can you ask what Tullia means by her sneer or her sniff when
    she passes
Modesty's ancient altar? One Moor-girl whispers to another,
Out of their litters they climb, and empty their bladders; the squirt-
    ing
Splashes the goddess's image. *It's my turn now! Let's play horsy!*
So in the light of the moon they are moved to the nastiest limits,
Then they go home, and you, on the way to greet your great friends
Early next day, soak your shoes in your wife's stale puddles of urine.

There's the Good Goddess, whose rites and mysteries scarcely are
    secrets,
Not when the flute music stirs the pelvis, and here they come sweep-
    ing,
Carried away by the horns and the wine, Priapus's maenads,
Tossing their manes and howling, craving, in absolute frenzy,
The beast with two backs, the gymnastics of lust, and their limbs
    fairly oozing
Passion's unmixed wine. Saufeia, in competition,
Wins the prize from them all, the slave girls who work for the pimps.
She swings a looser hip, but Medullina, in action,
Looses a juicier flow. So victory goes to the lady
Whose feats are as good as her birthright. This is no game, no
    pretense;
All of the actions here would make a Priapus of Priam,

Bring a burning heat to the cold old balls of a Nestor.
Now they cannot wait any more, they are utterly female,
Crying again and again, from every cranny and corner,
'Now is the proper time, now, now! Let the men come in!"
Maybe one gigolo is asleep; then send for another,
Let him put on a robe or a hood, but come in a hurry.
If there's nobody else, a slave will do; if no slaves
Are on hand, procure a water carrier, quickly;
If no human male is available, maybe a burro
Might, in time of need, supply what they want. How disgraceful!
Would that our ancient rites, at least in their public aspect,
Might be conducted without such evil, such blatant corruption.
But there's not a Moor in town, nor, for that matter, a Hindoo
Who doesn't know too well what lute player, said to be female,
Came with a tool twice the size of the Anti-Catos of Caesar
Into a place where a stud-mouse should scuttle away embarrassed,
Where even pictures of males are supposed to be covered with fig
     leaves.

Who ever sneered at the gods in the good old days? Who found
     Numa
A figure of fun, with his earthenware bowls, his black pots, or the
     brittle
Saucers of Vatican clay? But nowadays, where's the altar
Lacking its lute-playing fraud, its Clodius dressed like a woman?
Their appetites all are the same, no matter what class they have
     come from;
High or low, their lusts are alike; the barefooted woman
Treading the dark flagstone, the one tall Syrians carry
Litter-borne aloft—which is the better one? Neither!

In order to look at the games, Ogulnia hires herself clothes,
Hires attendants, a chair, cushions, girl friends, a nursemaid,
Also a blonde to run errands. All this is pretty expensive,
But if there's anything left of the family silver, she gives it,
The very last jug or jar in the house, to some athletic smoothie.
Many women like these are by no means well off. Does that matter?
None of them limits herself to the bounds that her poverty sets her.
None of them has any shame, any sense of decency. Sometimes
Men, at least, look ahead, are provident. *Go to the ant,*
Sluggard, consider her ways! They fear cold, therefore, and hunger,
But an extravagant woman has no idea whatsoever
That accounts can be overdrawn; she thinks that money is some-
　　thing
Like the mythical bird resurrected from its own ashes,
Something that grows on trees: why figure the cost of a pleasure?

In every house you will find a Professor of Obscene Matters.
Look at his right hand shake! He promises all kinds of doings.
Perverts all of them are, degraded, completely disgusting,
Yet they may spoil the bread, come to unholy communion;
The vessels are ordered washed, not smashed to bits as they should
　　be
After a Colocynth drinks, or a bearded Chelydon swallows.
So the man who conducts a training school for the wrestlers
Operates a house that is cleaner than yours is, more decent,
Seeing that his, at least, keeps the types away from each other,
Won't let the net-swishers join the ones with the spots on their
　　tunics,
Won't let the naked and armed keep their gear in a locker together.
The quarters reserved for the queers are the most remote from the
　　others

77

Both in the wrestling school and the jail, the gym and the prison.
But your wife makes you share the cup you drink from with creatures
Such as these, with whom a faded old whore from a graveyard
Would disdain to quaff wines of most exquisite vintage.
These are the seers they consult when they marry, or break off a
    marriage,
These are the ones with whom they relieve their spirits of boredom,
These are the ones who teach them movements of buttocks and
    pelvis
Or anything else they may know. But you cannot trust them com-
    pletely!
Better suspect the one who darkens his lashes with lampblack,
Puts on a saffron robe, and a woman's ribbons and hair net.
The softer his voice may be, and the more he rests his right hand
On his right hipbone and waggles his elbow a little,
The more this may all be put on, and in bed he's perfectly normal,
A champion, really, there, when he's put off the mask of a Thais,
Becoming the man with three—Wait! whom does he think he is
    fooling?
Put on this show for others, not me. I'd be willing to wager
He is really a man, completely a man. Do you doubt it,
Or shall I summon the maids and hear their detailed confession?
I know what you will say, and what all your old friends will advise
    you—
"Put a lock on the door: keep her in." But the question arises,
Who will be guarding the guards? They know enough to be silent,
They get paid in kind, and your wife has the cunning to know this,
Making her first misplays with the spies you have ordered to watch
    her.

There are some women who find unmanly eunuchs delightful,

Love the soft kisses of those who are hopeless of growing a beard—
No need here for precautions. But oh, the height of their pleasure
Comes when they happen on one who was fully mature when they
    took him
Off for the doctors to work on, and his quill was darkened already,
So what the surgeon removes hurts no one's game but the barber's
Once the members have grown, filled out, begun to weigh some-
    thing,
But if you get young boys, they really are wretchedly weakened,
Ashamed of their empty bag and the chick-peas that once were con-
    tained there.
This one, though, deprived, by his lady's will, of his manhood,
After his teens, is a noteworthy sight, outstanding Priapus
On his way to the baths. So, let him sleep with his lady,
But never let yourself think that he's impotent under the covers.

If she delights in song, she will make the professional singers
Come at her bidding; she holds their instruments in her hands,
While her sardonyx rings flash as her fingers are moving
Up and down the scale, and she holds the pick, and it quivers
As it used to do in the hand of the soft Hedymeles.
So she fondles it, finds it a joy and a consolation,
Gives it more than one kiss by way of endearing indulgence.
There was a lady descended, I think, from Appian nobles,
Yet she went with her wine and meal to Janus and Vesta
Asking them, goddess and god, whether Pollio, playing the lute,
Had any chance for the wreath of oak in the competition
Called the Capitol Games. What more could she possibly do
If her husband were sick, or the doctors anxious and gloomy
Over the case of her son? Yet there she stood by the altar
Thinking it no disgrace to veil her head for this lutester.

There she stood, repeating the ritual over and over,
All in due form, and turned pale as the lamb was being cut open.
Janus, most ancient of gods, Janus, most reverend father,
Tell me, can people like these expect any answers from Heaven?
Gods must have little to do, I guess, and suffer from boredom.
While one lady consults you about some ridiculous comic,
While another one seeks your favor for some tragic ham,
What will the soothsayer get but varicose veins for his patience?

Better to let her sing than be running all over the city,
Bold as a man, attending the meetings of men, with her husband
One of the throng, while she holds forth, hard-faced and dry-
     breasted,
Talking with all the High Brass. She knows the classified secrets
Of the whole wide world, what the Russians and Chinese are up to,
Knows, furthermore, what goes on between stepmother and stepson,
Who is in love with whom, which swordsman is all the rage,
Who made the widow pregnant, and in what month; and she also
Knows what endearments they use, women in bed with their lovers,
Also what methods they use. She sees, before any others,
The comet that threatens the king, of Parthia, say, or Armenia.
She is the first to hear, at the city gates, all the rumors
Recently come to town and she has been known to invent them,
Saying Niphates is pouring in flood over cities and people—
(This is a mountain, of course, but she has it mixed up with a
     river)—
Over the fields, overwhelming the earth: she chatters the story
Into any ear she encounters at any street corner.

This is no harder to bear than the way she treats her poor neighbors
Cutting them down with the lash, no matter how they entreat her.

If she is sound asleep, and a dog awakes her by barking,
"Hurry up with the whip!" she cries. And who is the victim?
Oh, the poor dog, of course; but his turn comes after his master's.
She is a menace to meet and worse than disaster to look at.
She goes to the baths at night, at night she demands her canteens,
Mess kits, oil flasks, all the gear of her camping equipment.
There she loves to sweat, with the din and bustle about her.
When her arms are tired from lifting the weights or the dumbbells,
Then it is time for the man with the oil to give her a rubdown.
Don't think that's all he does—his fingers are certainly clever,
Knowing where they can go, and how they can work up a climax.
Meanwhile her pitiful guests are waiting, waiting forever,
So it would seem, half-dead with sleep, exhausted and hungry.
Finally here she comes, all red in the face, dry-throated,
Thirsty enough to swig at least a couple of gallons
With a pint or two for a chaser, something to make her real hungry.
She cannot hold this down; the floor is presently flooded,
Streams run over the marble; a reek of Falernian wine
Rises strong in the air as the golden vessel runs over.
So she drinks, or pukes, as a long snake does when he tumbles
Into a cask or a vat. Her husband feels the same impulse,
Closes his eyes and succeeds in keeping his bile down, but barely.

Even worse is the one who has scarcely sat down at the table
When she starts in on books, with praise for Virgil and pardon
For the way Dido died; she makes comparisons, placing
Virgil one side of the scales, and counterweights him with Homer.
Critics surrender, professors are lost; the whole crowd is silent.
No one can get in a word edgewise, not even a lawyer,
No, nor an auctioneer, nor even another woman,
Such is the force of her words, the syllables pouring in torrents

Making a din like that when pots and kettles are rattled
In an eclipse of the moon. No need of trumpets or cymbals,
All by herself she can make all of the noise that is needed.
What a philosopher, too, with her definitions of morals!
What she ought to do, since she wants to seem eloquent, learned,
Is to tuck up her skirts to her knees and bring to Sylvanus
(Women may not do this) a little pig as an offering,
Or go to the penny baths, the ones the philosophers frequent,
The only ones they can afford, along with the general public.
Postumus, my good friend, don't let the wife of your bosom
Ever acquire the style of an orator, whirling the sentence,
Heaving the enthymeme, or the undistributed middle.
Don't let her know too much about historical matters,
Let there be some things in books she does not understand. How I
    hate them,
Women who always go back to the pages of Palaemon's grammar,
Keeping all of the rules, and are pedants enough to be quoting
Verses I never heard. If she has some friend from the country
Let her correct her speech! Is this a business for men?
Husbands should be allowed their solecisms in comfort!

There's nothing a woman won't do, nothing she thinks is disgraceful
With the green gems at her neck, or pearls distending her ear !obes.
Nothing is worse to endure than your Mrs. Richbitch, whose visage
Is padded and plastered with dough, in the most ridiculous manner.
Furthermore, she reeks of unguents, so God help her husband
With his wretched face stunk up with these, smeared by her lipstick
To her lovers she comes with her skin washed clean. But at home
Why does she need to look pretty? Nard is assumed for the lover,
For the lover she buys all the Arabian perfumes.
It takes her some time to strip down to her face, removing the layers

One by one, till at last she is recognizable, almost,
Then she uses a lotion, she-asses' milk; she'd need herds
Of these creatures to keep her supplied on her northernmost jour-
    neys.
But when she's given herself the treatment in full, from the ground
    base
Through the last layer of mud pack, from the first wash to a poultice,
What lies under all this—a human face, or an ulcer?

It might be well worth your while to have a good look at these ladies,
How they keep busy all day. But consider the nighttime before this:
If the husband has slept with his back to the lady, tough luck
For the woman who cards the wool, tough luck for the tiring women,
Tough luck for the man with the litter: the sleep of the husband
    will cost them
Plenty of grief, the rod for one, the strap for another,
The lash for a third: some women save money by paying their flog-
    gers
Not by the job but the year—an annual basis is cheaper.
Whipping's no bother at all: she can smear her face while it hap-
    pens,
Listen to female friends, or study the flounce of a garment.
Crack goes the whip! She reads the Daily News, every column.
Crack goes the whip! But at last they grow tired, and she growls,
    "Oh, get out!"
For one day, at least, the investigation is over.

No Sicilian court is more unjust than her household
If she has made a decision, and wants to appear more becoming
Than her usual style, in a hurry to get to the gardens
Where her somebody waits, or to get to the temple of Isis

83

(Brothel would be more like it), her hair is put up by a handmaid,
Psecas by name, with her own hair a mess, and naked of shoulder,
Naked of breasts. "Why won't this curl lie flat?" And the cowhide
Takes it out on the maid because of the lack of a cowlick.
Why was that Psecas' fault? Or how in the world could she help it
If the lady found the shape of her own nose disgusting?
Another maid needs both hands to comb her hair and to coil it,
Then there's one more on the staff, who used to work for her mother,
Now more or less retired, but first to express her opinion
By seniority's right; let the younger or awkwarder follow
Taking the floor in due course, as if we had here great questions
Of church or of state, of life or death, not merely the problem
Of the build-up of beauty, hair skyscraper-high on the head.
Look at her from the front—that must be Andromache, surely!
But from the rear she seems a good deal more like a midget.
What can she do if the luck of the draw has assigned her dimen-
     sions,
Given her half-pint size, which even high heels can't correct,
So that she has to jump straight up in the air for her kisses?
Meanwhile, she takes no thought for her husband, or what she must
     cost him,
More like a neighbor than wife, and intimate only in hating
Both his friends and his slaves, and in running up bills.

                                              Here they come,
The choirs of Bellona the wild, of Cybele, and one big eunuch
Whose countenance calls for awe from lesser obscene devotees,
Seeing he once, long ago, cut off his own balls with a sharp shell.
Now the noisy rout gives way, and the drums defer,
As, with a Phrygian's headdress veiling his commoner's features,
In a solemn voice, he warns her, Beware of September,

Beware of the hurricanes, unless she has made an oblation,
First, of a hundred eggs, or given him some old garments
The color of vine leaves in autumn, by way of preventive magic
Whereby what danger there is, however appalling or sudden,
Passes into the clothes, a full year's expiation.
On a winter day she will go down to the Tiber,
Break the morning ice, plunge three times into the current,
Wash her fearful head where the waves crest high, and then, trem-
    bling,
Naked, with bleeding knees, crawl out on the field of Mars.
If white Io commands, she will go to the borders of Egypt,
Fetch from the sun-warmed Nile water, and sprinkle the temple
Sacred to Isis, that stands near the polling booths of the city.
She has no doubt that she's called by the actual voice of the god-
    dess—
What a fine soul and mind for the gods to talk with by nighttime!—
Here the highest of praise is due to the dog-headed god
Who with his linen-clad, bald-headed throng of attendants
Runs along and laughs at the grief of the people, Anubis,
Intercessor for wives who pollute the sheets with embraces
On the holiest days and must pay for this violation.
Heavy payment due, if ever the silver serpent
Seems to have nodded his head! But tears, the rehearsal of murmurs,
Prove that pardon will come, a big goose will insure absolution,
Or a little wafer suffice to win over Osiris.

Well, this fellow has gone. The next to come is a Jewess
Leaving her basket and hay, soliciting alms, all a-tremble,
Claiming she knows the laws of Jerusalem. This High Priestess
Has to live under a tree, but she knows all the secrets of Heaven.
She, too, will fill her palm, but not too full; a few coppers

Purchase, where Jews are concerned, fulfillment of dreams and
    fancies.

A Commagenian seer or Armenian fortuneteller
Will promise you tender young love or bequests that are handsome
After inspecting the lungs of a dove or the crop of a chicken
Or the entrails of a puppy or maybe even a child's.
He will do some things for the sake of turning informer,
But the Chaldean seers are apparently more to be trusted.
What those astrologers say appears to come straight from the
    sources
Hammon inspires, since Delphi is dumb, and a darkness
Falls on the human race when it comes to knowing the future.
Not the least of these is one who was often an exile,
By whose friendship (for sale) and equally venal divining
That great citizen fell, the emperor dreaded by Otho.
Fellows like these are believed if they've been in some far-off prison,
Shackled hand and foot: if he hasn't a prison record,
Then he has no renown, but a sentence to one of the islands,
A narrow escape from death, procures him a reputation.
These are the ones your wife, like Tanaquil, truly an expert,
Goes to consult: how soon will her mother die of the jaundice?
(She asked about your last hour long ago.) And when will she bury
Her sister, her uncles? How long will her present lover survive her?
So far, she can't understand the gloomy portents of Saturn
Or beneath what star Venus reveals herself joyous,
Which are the losing months, and which the seasons for winners.
Don't forget to duck when you meet with one of these women
Clutching no amber beads to keep her palms from perspiring,
But a calendar worn till she's hardly able to read it.
She is an expert herself, giving, not given, advices.

If her husband goes to the wars or returns to his homeland,
She will not be at his side if the runes of Thrasyllus forbid it.
If she wants to take a short ride out of the city,
She has to look up in her book to find out what hour is propitious.
If she has an itch when she rubs an eye, she will never
Think of applying salve till the horoscope's been consulted.
If she lies sick in bed, she will take no food till she figures
What is the right time to eat, as per Petosiris' directions.

If she is not too well off, she will travel around the Circus
Where they draw lots; she will find a phrenologist there, or a palm-
    ist
(Not so expensive perhaps, but at least the turnover's frequent),
But your rich women hire imported Phrygian augurs,
Said to be most sage in the ways of the constellations,
Or those wise old men who purify ground struck by lightning.
Poverty learns its fates at the Circus, or Servian rampart;
Women whose shoulders are bare, wearing the long gold necklace,
Go to the posts of the Dolphin or Egg, the Blue or the Green, to
    discover
Whether to jilt the barkeep, or marry the old-clothes peddler.

Yet these women at least endure the perils of childbirth,
Suffer the nuisance of nursing—but when did you ever discover
Labor pains in a golden bed? There are potent prescriptions,
Fine professional skill, to be hired for inducing abortions,
Killing mankind in the womb. Rejoice, unfortunate husband,
Give her the dose yourself, whatever it is; never let her
Carry till quickening time, or go on to full term and deliver
Something whose hue would seem to prove you a blackamoor father,
Sire of an off-color heir you'd prefer not to meet in the daylight.

I will not mention the children set out to die from exposure,
Hopes and prayers deceived, the pools and the filthy waters
Whence our ministers come, our dancing priests, the deluded
Bearers of noble names, as often as not poor bastards,
Seeing that Fortune, by night, is shameless and smiles on the chil-
    dren,
Fondles them all, and folds them to her, and then, for amusement,
Lets them go to the homes of the great, and loves them, and, smil-
    ing,
Gives them her blessing, her best, and sets them above all the others.

Here comes a quack with magical spells to peddle a wife, and an-
    other
Selling Thessalian charms whose effect on the mind of a husband
Proves so strong his wife can paddle his ass with a slipper,
Chump that he is, but perhaps just as well, if he cannot remember
Deeds of the day before, with this darkness of spirit upon him.
Things could be worse: he might be like Nero's uncle, for instance,
Stark and staring mad, from the potion Caesonia mixed him.
What won't a woman do, if an empress sets the example?
All things went up in flames, and all things came down in ruins
Just as if Juno herself had driven her husband to madness.
Agrippina, it seems, was not so bad with her mushrooms
Telling one silly and drooling old man to descend to the heavens,
But Caesonia's draft brought fire and the sword and the rack,
Mixed the blood of the knights and the blood of the senate together,
Such was the power of that brew, the power of one murderous
    woman.

Women, of course, are right to hate the sons of a rival;
No one should cavil at that, it's a custom of ancient tradition,

Killing a stepson, I mean, and perfectly normal and proper.
But you adopted sons, with more than ample possessions,
Take my advice, look out for your lives, trust none of the dishes.
Those potpies are black with poisons put there by mother.
Let somebody else taste first of whatever she offers,
Pass your tutor the cup, and don't be surprised if he shudders.

Of course I am making this up, and my Muse is assuming, too
    grandly,
Tragedy's buskin and mask. Do you think so? think that my trespass
Steps beyond limits and bounds of precedent? think I am crazy,
Crazy, or drunk, and mouthing a theme, in Sophocles' manner,
Foreign to Latin skies and Rutulian mountain and woodland?
Would that I were so wrong! But here is Pontia crying
"I did it, I confess, I gave my children the poison,
Did it with my own hands, and nothing secret about it!"
"Two at one sitting, you viper, you fiend, you vilest of women,
Two at one sitting?" "Of course, and seven if there had been seven."

Let us believe what they tell us about Medea and Procne;
No use denying the fact. Those women were monsters of daring
In their own day, but their crimes were not committed for money.
It is not so strange when women find their incentive
To their evil deeds in a passionate anger that bears them
Down like a rock torn loose from the crumbling side of a mountain
When the ground gives way, and a chasm splits from the hillside.
The woman I cannot stand is the calculating woman
Committing her crimes in cold blood. Our wives consider Alcestis
Taking her husband's fate upon her; given the freedom,
They'd like a husband to die to save the life of their lap dog.
Every morning, in Rome, you'll meet the daughters of Belus,

More than one Eriphyle, and almost every apartment
Is Clytemnestra's address. In one respect only they differ—
She used a two-edged axe, our girls toad-poison or mushroom.
Still, it might be well if they practiced, a little, with weapons.
Possibly one of these days the husbands will take some precautions,
Making themselves immune in the manner of Mithridates.

On poets, pedagogues, and poverty

WHATEVER hope we have, whatever inducement to study
Rests on Caesar alone, the Muses' only respecter
In these sorrowful days, when poets of high reputation,
In order to make a few cents, think of a bath concession
In some little town like Gabii, think of a bakeshop
Here in Rome, or perhaps try crying the sales at an auction.
None too great a disgrace, after all; any one of the Muses,
Starving, could hardly be blamed for leaving Helicon's fountains
In hot haste for a job in the auction rooms of the city,
More or less content with Machaera's trade and his profits,
Bawling, "Going! Gone!" over wine casks, bookcases, tripods,
Copies of plays, for example the *Thebes* or *Tereus* of Faustus,

Paccius' masterpiece, the one about Minyas' daughter
Changed to a bat. A better career, to be sure, than appearing
In some police-court case, claiming you saw what you did not.
Leave all that to our new-made knights, the ex-slaves from Asia,
Cappadocia, Gaul, with the chalk marks still on their ankles.

Nobody, from now on, no bard who has nibbled the laurel,
No one who ever bound words to melodious measures
Ever will have to submit to employment unworthy his calling.
On with your work, young men! Your prince, your patron, is watch-
     ing,
Urging you to produce material worth his indulgence.
If you have any idea of waiting for some other fellow
To come to your aid, Telesinus, and any such hope keeps you filling
Foolscap, ream upon ream, you would be better off if you ordered
Plenty of kindling wood, and presented your product to Vulcan
Or put the volumes away in a cupboard, a feast for the bookworms.
Break your pen, poor wretch; destroy those epics of battles
Costing you sleepless nights, the lofty hymns of the garret,
The hope of the scraggy bust and the stringy garland of ivy.
That is the best you can hope for, no more. Our rich men are misers
Willing to give three cheers, like boys admiring a peacock
(This doesn't cost them a cent), for the eloquent verse of the poets.
Meanwhile your prime of life, your hardihood, your endurance
Wherewith you might have been a soldier or sailor or farmer
Goes to its ebb, and the spirit lags, and a worn-out old age,
Eloquent, but in rags, hates itself and its art.

Don't forsake the shrine where the Muses dwell, and Apollo,
In any hope you can find a private patron to help you.
He writes verses himself, of course, and will grant you that Homer,

After a thousand years, has a following somewhat greater.
Don't assume from this that he has any sympathy in him
For the bards of today. Here is how he will work it.
If the desire for fame leads you to give a recital,
He will find you a hall, or a house all falling to pieces,
Out of the way, with the front door barred like the gate of a sieged
    town.
He will supply a claque, his freedmen along the aisles,
But he won't give you a cent to hire the benches they sit on,
Not a cent for the chairs arranged on the lecture platform,
Not a cent for the front-row seats you send back to the owner
After the program ends. But still we're persistent, we poets,
Ploughing our furrows in dust or the salty sand of the seashore.
No use to try to give up; the noose of a hopeless infection,
Writer's itch, has us all by the neck till we're old and sick-hearted.

But your distinguished bard, whose talent is far from the common,
Who speaks to the point, avoiding the trite and the long-drawn-out,
Your genuine poet—I'm sorry I can't show you one, I am only
Sure he exists—is made with a spirit untroubled by anguish,
Unembittered, serene, fond of the woodlands, and worthy
To drink at the Muses' fount. But Poverty isn't a singer—
How can you sing in the grot when you haven't a cent in your
    pockets?
How can you flourish the wand when you're hungry and thirsty and
    gloomy
All of the night and all of the day? *Rejoice!* Horace told us.
This is all very well—but Horace had a full belly.
Where can talent find a place except where the spirit
Truly cares for song, and no ambivalent feelings
Trouble the heart whose lord is Apollo, or Dionysus?

Not from some cheap little mind concerned with the cost of a
      blanket,
But from a lofty soul arise those visions of godhead,
Chariots, riders and steeds, and the Fury dashing at Turnus.
Virgil, without at least one slave, and a decent apartment,
Never could bring to life the terrible blast of her trumpet
Or the snakes of her hair. Imagine a bald-headed Fury!
Is it fair to suppose Rubrenus Lappa, for instance,
Hard at work on his play, the *Atreus,* ever will tower
Over the ancient composers of tragedy? Not bloody likely,
Not while he has to hock his cloak and his dishes for paper.
Numitor—now there's a patron! The poor unfortunate fellow
Has nothing to give to a friend, but only to send to his mistress.
He could scrape up enough, it seems, to feed a tame lion—
Everybody knows a lion eats less than a poet.

Lucan may lie content with his fame, content in those gardens
Where his statues rise, but is glory ever sufficient,
Glory alone, for men like Serranus or Saleius Bassus?
All the people turn out in droves, and hear, with rejoicing,
Statius' beautiful voice, as he keeps his promise and reads them
Lines from his epic on Thebes. There's not a dry seat in the house.
Statius, however, will starve unless he can manage to peddle
His Agave, thus far unpublished, but suitable, maybe, for Paris,
Paris, our patron saint, Paris the pantomimist.
He has the power to secure you title and rank in the army
Honorary, of course, and a golden ring on your finger
Proving you've served six months. Paris the actor will give you
More than a nobleman does; so why hang around in their hallways?
One leading lady (male) appoints our prefects, another
Nominates our tribunes, Pelopea or Philomela.

Do not envy the poet supplied, through the stage, with a living.
Who, in these days, will there be to play to role of Maecenas,
Patron of art, the friend of Propertius, Horace, and Virgil?
That was the time when genius was given its due, and a poet
Found it well worth while to work through the holiday revels.

Are you so much better off, O writer of history? Surely
You waste more time and more oil and thousands of pages of paper
Costing a fortune: still, the laws of the craft are demanding,
What with footnotes and research, cross references and index.
But how does the harvest pay off? What profit in all of this delv-
    ing?
What historian gets as much as a clerk in a courtroom?
"Oh, but they're lazy slobs, who delight in the shade and the chaise
    longue."
How about lawyers, then, who bustle about in the courtroom
Loaded with briefs? How they do sound off, with their creditors
    watching!
Not to mention the act they put on if they've gotten a nudge
From some prospect, whose case appears exceedingly doubtful.
What big lies they puff out as they heave and pant like a bellows
Drooling all over their chins and halfway down to their navels!
Yet, if you'd like the facts of their income, a hundred lawyers
Hardly make as much as that Red race driver, The Lizard.
The leaders are seated, and you are rising to argue, like Ajax,
Only a lot more pale, for a client whose freedom's in question,
In the court of some clodhopping judge. Bust a gut, you poor
    sucker,
What will you get? Worn out, and the major reward for your labors
Green palm leaves on the garret stairs, and perhaps, in addition,
A shrivelled-up ham, a can of sardines, some veteran onions

That would feed a Moor for a month, bad wine from up Tiber, five
    bottles.
After four briefs, you get one gold piece, all but the fraction
Which, as you know, accrues to a few of your fee-splitting colleagues.
If he comes from the ranks of the nobles, any attorney
Gets the maximum fee, though ours is a better performance.
Still he has in his courtyard four horses hauling a chariot
All of bronze, and himself riding on one of them, fiercely
Flapping a bending spear, half-blind, or should we say cockeyed?
That's how Pedo goes broke, and Matho is always in trouble.
Such will be the end of Tongilius, haunting the baths
With his oil flask of rhinoceros horn and his filthy retainers,
Maedians, weighted down under the poles of his litter
As through the forum he rides to purchase slave boys or silver,
Red and white agate, a country estate. That Tyrian purple,
Worn on a lawyer's back, brings him both credit and clients.
This is what pays off, to live in continual uproar
Always beyond one's means; Rome puts no limit on spending.

Trust in eloquence, then? Cicero would not be given
Even a minimum fee, if he wore no ring on his finger.
If a man's going to law, the first thing he has to consider
Is, do you have eight slaves, a litter, companions in togas
Walking ahead as you go? When Paulus pleaded his cases,
He wore a ring he had hired, a spectacular gem of sardonyx,
That's why his fees were more than those of attorneys like Gallus.
Eloquence seldom is found when a counselor's wardrobe is shabby.
When can a Basilus move the court with the tears of a mother?
Who would listen to him, no matter how well he was speaking?
Better be off to Gaul, or to Africa, mother of lawyers,
If you suppose that your tongue is going to earn you a living.

Or do you teach declamation? What iron nerve must be needed
While your class, by the score, knocks off tyrannical monarchs.
Each schoolboy, in turn, gets up, and, standing, delivers
What he's just read sitting down, in the most monotonous singsong.
This is the kind of rehash that kills unfortunate masters.
What kind of case do we have? What's the best side to develop?
What refutation will come from the speech of the opposition?
That's what they all want to know, but no one is willing to pay
    for.
"Pay you? But what have I learned?"—it's always the fault of the
    teacher
If his scholars aren't thrilled to the core of their moronic beings
Every sixth day when they bore us to death with the villain from
    Carthage,
What he debates in his mind, whether to capture the city
After his triumph at Cannae, or lead his cohorts with caution,
Soaked to the skin as they are from war's grim tempest and deluge.
Name what amount you please—I'd be perfectly willing to pay it
If the boys' fathers would hear their orations as often as I do.
That's the common cry from our teachers, almost by the dozens,
As they go to court for their fees, as they must, forgetting the
    speeches
Dealing with Tarquin the Proud, with Medea, or possibly Jason,
Or the one about drugs that restore the vision to blind men.
So, my advice would be, if any one's willing to listen,
Live a different life, come down from rhetoric's shadow
Into the sun of the games, get one fight, take your payment in pea-
    nuts,
Then announce your retirement, go into some other profession.
Try to find out what it costs to hire an instructor in music
For the smart set's sons; then tear up your *How to Teach Speaking!*

97

Your great lord spends thousands, or more than that, on his bath-
     rooms,
And even more fanciful sums on places to dine when it's rainy.
Don't think he'll wait for the sun, or let his ponies get muddy.
Better to ride where the gilded hoofs will always shine brightly.
Somewhere he has a banqueting hall with Numidian columns
Catching the winter sun. How much did this cost? What a question!
He can still afford a cook and a table setter,
Specialists, both, in their art. Well then, how much for Quintilian?
(Nothing a father won't pay when it comes to a son's education.)
Five or ten bucks. "But Quintilian," you say, "appears to have
     plenty!"
Never mind; let it go. Rules always have their exceptions.
If you are lucky, you're brave, you're wise, you're noble, you're hand-
     some,
You can wear black shoes with the senatorial crescent.
If you are lucky, you hurl the javelin farther than any,
Make the greatest orations, and even with laryngitis
Sing like an angel. The stars must be in the proper conjunction—
Nothing else matters as much—at the time when, red as a lobster,
Fresh from your mother's womb, you first give out with your squal-
     ling.
Luck may be kind: you will be a consul instead of a teacher.
Luck may change her mind: you're a teacher again, not a consul.
Bassus and Cicero rose from nowhere and nothing. What brought
     them
High, save the power of the stars, and the secret wonders of Fortune?
Fortune makes kings of slaves and gives the captive a triumph,
Yet the fortunate man is very much harder to come on
Than a white crow. And it often turns out that the chairs of profes-
     sors

Prove a delusion and snare. The case of Thrasymachus proves it;
And there have been others, no doubt—for instance, the teacher in
    Athens
Whom his citizens blessed with the goblet of ice-cold hemlock.
Gods, may the earth be soft and light on the shades of our fathers,
The crocus bloom, and spring be eternal over their ashes.
They were men who revered a teacher as much as a parent.
Achilles, fully grown up, feared the rod and respected
Chiron the Centaur, who taught him song in his native mountains.
But what happens today? More than one teacher, like Rufus,
"Cicero of the Rhone," is beaten up by his pupils.
Who pays the learned Palaemon, or Celadus, what they deserve?
Yet, of the little they get, the scholar's nitwit attendant
Has to take his cut, and so does the steward disburser.
Might as well give up, Palaemon. A blanket seller
Knocks a little off for a white sale during the winter.
Just so you get some pay, however little, for sitting
All night long in some dump no blacksmith would ever put up with,
In some dump that would choke the meanest wool-carder's appren-
    tice.
Just so you get some pay for inhaling the reek of the lamps,
One for each boy in the class, with their Horace completely discol-
    ored
And the Virgilian pages grimy and sooty with lampblack.
Just so you get some pay—but for that it takes a court order.

But, you parents, impose the strictest rules on the teacher.
Insist that his usage of words is precise, that he knows all the classics
Like his own fingers and toes, that he's learned in history, also.
If he's on his way to the baths, don't let him go till he tells you
Who was Anchises' nurse, or where Anchemolus's stepmother

Came from, and what was her name, and what was the age of
    Acestes,
Also how many casks of wine he bestowed on the Trojans.
Make him mold their young minds, as a man models faces from
    beeswax,
Keeping them under his thumb, and be looked upon as a father,
Not let them play dirty tricks, or develop the nastier habits.
It is no easy task to keep your eye on the students,
Watching the hands and the eyes of the impudent mischievous
    devils.
"That's your job," they say, and your pay, at the end of a twelve-
    month,
Equals a jockey's fee if he's ridden only one winner.

Against base nobles

WHAT good are family trees? Oh, Ponticus, what's the advantage
In your ancient blood, in having the family statues
Placed all about in your halls, and more or less going to pieces,
Aemilius in his car, Curius crumbling, Corvinus
Lacking a shoulder, and Galba worse off, with no nose and no ears?
What is the profit with men like these in a branch of the household,
Dictators, Masters of Horse, dim with the dust of the ages?
Where does the profit lie, if your life is devoted to evil
Almost before their eyes? What good are the statues of heroes
If you spend all night throwing dice, and not until daybreak
Start for your bed, at an hour when your warrior ancestors ordered
Camp to be moved and the march to go forward? Here is a fellow

Sprung from Hercules' line, a Fabius—how does he dare be
Proud of the conqueror's title bestowed, or of the Great Altar,
Hercules' own, if he's silly, and avaricious, and softer
Than a Euganean lamb? The chests of his forebears were hairy;
Look at him, though, with his butt all smoothed by Catanian pum-
     ice!
How dare he be proud, a buyer of poison, convicted,
Bringing disgrace on the house, and a statue the law orders broken.
Statues may fill your halls from one end to the other, but Virtue,
Virtue alone is proof of nobility. Act like a Cossus,
Paulus or Drusus; behave like them; defer to their statues
More than those of your house, and even when you are consul
Honor them more than your rank. Your primary obligation
Lies in goodness of soul. Are you really deserving of honor,
Holding fast to the just in word and deed? I proclaim you
Nobleman, then. All hail, whatever your birth! The Egyptians
Cry, when Osiris is born, "We have found him; rejoice!" So our peo-
     ple
Cheer when they find, for once, a citizen rare and distinguished.
True nobility lies in more than a name and a title.
We call somebody's dwarf an *Atlas*; his black boy is *Swansdown*,
We label some ugly lopsided girl *Europa*; and mongrels,
Mangy and worthless, the kind that try to lick oil from dry vessels,
We call *Lion*, or *Tiger*, or *Pard*, or whatever roars loudest.
So, beware lest your title is given in any such spirit,
Lest "The Victor of Crete" means Crete's where you took such a
     beating.

For whom is my warning meant? For you, Rubellius Blandus.
You are all swollen up because you're descended from Drusus.
What is your actual claim to be considered a noble?

Is it getting yourself conceived from the shining line of Iulus,

Not by some wench who spins for hire at the base of the windy
    walls?

"You are the dregs," you say, "the scum of the earth, the rabble.

There's not a man of you all who can show where his father was lit-
    tered,

But I come down from the kings!" Long life to you, Sire, and long
    pleasure

In your illustrious birth! And yet, from among the plebeians,

From this common herd, you will find the eloquent Roman

Able to plead the cause of the barbarous ignorant noble.

From the common folk will arise the solver of riddles,

Breaker of legal knots; from them will emerge the young soldier

Active in arms, on the march with the eagles to distant Euphrates,

While you sit at home, a Hermes, armless and legless,

What a comedown from the kings! Over Hermes you have one ad-
    vantage:

He has a marble head, while yours, though empty, is living.

Tell me, son of the Trojans: in the case of dumb beasts, does it
    matter

How they are bred, if they're strong? We praise a race horse for
    running,

Burning speed, and the roar of the crowd as he comes home a win-
    ner.

He is the thoroughbred, no matter what pasture he fed on,

Who can get the job done, and the others dusty behind him.

But if he never wins, let the dray or the glue factory claim him,

Though his sire may have been Man of War, Native Dancer, Nas-
    rullah.

What does the race track care for pedigreed phantoms and shadows?

All those heavy of foot might as well be pounding the treadmill,
Making the wheels go round, galling their necks with the collar,
Changing masters, obeying, and always cheaper and cheaper.
So, if you want our respect for your worth and not your possessions,
Give us something your own, some personal proof of your title
Going beyond the claims of our past and present allegiance
To those ancestors in whose debt you are fully indentured.

This is enough for the youth puffed up, according to rumor,
From the fact that he claims to be a relation of Nero's.
In that walk of life, a decent feeling for others
Seldom, if ever, is found. Therefore, my Ponticus, do not
Covet praise for your birth, yourself contributing nothing.
Shaky indeed is the prop if you lean on the glory of others;
The house will come tumbling down, the columns shatter in ruins.
Low on the ground, the vine longs for the elm it deserted.
Be a good soldier, be good to your ward, be a person of honor.
If you are summoned to court, in a case uncertain and doubtful,
Even though Phalaris threatens and brings up his bull to suborn
    you,
Tell no lie, believe that the worst sin of all is preferring
Life to honor; don't lose, for life's sake, your reasons for living.
If a man is worthy of death, he is dead, though he banquets on
    oysters,
Though he bathes in a tub that reeks with the perfumes of Cosmos.

When at last you leave to go out to govern your province,
Limit your anger and greed; pity our destitute allies,
Whose poor bones you see sucked dry of their pith and their mar-
    row.
Have respect for the law, respect the Senate's instruction,

Keep in mind the rewards of the god, the blast of the lightning
Hurled by the Senate's arm against the Cilician pirates.
Yet what good is all this, if one robber replaces another?
All the poor native can do is peddle what rags he has left,
Keep his mouth shut, and hope he won't lose his passage money
Whether to Rome or to Hell.
　　　　　　　　　　　　It was different once. In the old days
What our allies lost would cost them sorrow and groaning
Over their wounds, to be sure, but then they were flourishing cities,
They had only been beaten, not put to the last desolation.
Every home was well-stocked, and the men had plenty of money,
Spartan cloaks, Coan silks, Parrhasian paintings, and statues,
The workmanship of the best, Polyclitus, Phidias, Myron.
Hardly a table was set without some silver by Mentor.
Then Dolabella came, Antony, infamous Verres,
All of them loading tall ships with private spoil, and more trophies
Taken in peace than in war. Today, if you capture a farmhouse,
You get a few yoke of oxen, a few brood mares, and one stud-horse.
As for the household gods, there might be one statue worth stealing,
One little god from one little shrine to make do, as a makeshift.
Possibly you despise unwarlike Rhodes, perfumed Corinth.
You are perfectly right, of course; what harm can be done you
By young men who shave not only their shins but their armpits?
But keep away from Spain, it's rugged there; keep away from
Gaul and the Yugoslav coast; don't bother those African gleaners
Stuffing the gut of the city whose care is the stage and the Circus.
Come to think of it, though, they have little left to be taken.
Marius, not long since, stripped them right down to their loincloths.
Here's the first rule: don't harm men who have nothing but courage.
Stripped of their silver and gold, they still rely on their weapons,
Shields and helmets and swords and javelins of the spirit.

What I have just set forth is no mere slogan, believe me.
This is the absolute truth; I am reading the leaves of the Sibyl.
If your whole staff consists of men you can trust, if no longhair
Has your decisions for sale, if your wife is above suspicion,
Not like a harpy with talons, ready to pounce on the money
Whether in country or town, then you can trust your descent
All the way back to Picus, or if lofty names please you better,
Call yourself son of the Giants, the Titans, or even Prometheus.
But if ambition and lust seize on you, carry you headlong,
If you break the rods on the bloody backs of our allies,
If you're in love with axes worn dull, and headsmen exhausted,
Then your family pride begins to rise up and reproach you
Throwing the light of the torch on deeds too shameful to mention.
Every vice of the soul calls obloquy down on the sinner
In direct ratio to his title and reputation.
What do I care for the temples your grandfather built, where your
    father
Has a triumphal statue, if that's the place you resort to
For your forging of records? How does the family virtue
Matter to me, if you sneak out at night with your countenance hid-
    den
Under a Gallic hood, on some adulterous mission?

Driving at breakneck speed past the ashes and bones of his fathers
Whirls Lateranus the fat, a mule skinner once, now a consul,
Setting the brake on the wheel in his old professional manner.
This is at night, to be sure, but the moon looks on, and the planets
Strain their wondering eyes. When his term of office is over,
Lateranus won't mind taking his whip in broad daylight,
Greeting old friends with a flick of the lash, untying the hay bales
With his own hands, giving out the barley and oats to his horses.

Meanwhile, though he performs the rites in the manner of Numa,
Slaying oxen and lambs, even at Jove's high altar,
He swears by no other god than Hippona, mistress of horseflesh
And those faces that hang on the smelly walls of the tack room.
When he decides to go to some tavern that never closes,
On his way he is met by a perfumed Syrophoenician,
Coming up at a run, to hail him as lord and master
With all the airs of a host, and with him a woman, Cyane,
Skirts hiked up to her knees, and her bottle ready to peddle.

"Young men will sow their wild oats," I can hear some indulgent old
    fellow
Making excuses, "We acted the same way when we were boys."
Maybe you did, but you managed to stop, and were foolish no
    longer.
Let the time be brief for bold and shameful behavior;
Cut off delinquent days when you first cut your juvenile whiskers.
Boys rate a certain amount of indulgence, but this Lateranus,
Running around to the grogshops under their awnings of linen,
Surely was old enough for the wars, for guarding the rivers
In Armenian lands or Syrian, Danube or Rhine.
He was old enough to protect the person of Nero.
Send to Ostia, Caesar; there you will find your lieutenant
If you have the search conducted in some big cookshop.
There you will find him, sprawled out with gangsters of every de-
    scription,
Runaway slaves and sailors and thieves and coffin-makers and butch-
    ers,
Or a eunuch priest on his back in the midst of his cymbals.
Freedom for all! And all things in common, the cup and the table,
Not to mention the bed. Ah, Ponticus, how would you treat him,

This kind of slave? I am sure you would pack him off to some jail-
 house,
Out in the countryside, to work with others in field gangs.
But you pardon yourselves, you gentry, Trojan-descended,
Give yourselves license for acts that the working classes would blush
 at.

I find it hard to produce examples so vile and disgusting
There's not a worse left unmentioned. When all of his future was
 squandered
Damasippus hired out to play the Loud Ghost, of Catullus.
Lentulus took the role of the highwayman born to be hanged;
There was typecasting for you! Don't be too soft on the people,
They are partly to blame as they sit there, brazenfaced, staring,
Watching patricians clown, the sons of a Fabius barefoot,
Numa's descendants—what fun!—clouting each other with slap-
 sticks.
How cheap can you get? And who cares? Yet no tyrannical Nero
Makes them sell themselves at the games of His Highness the
 praetor.
But imagine you did have to choose: on the one hand, death; on the
 other,
Playing a part on the stage, a clown or a cuckolded husband,
Which is the nobler way out? Is death such an absolute horror?
Still, when the emperor turns to playing a fiddle, no wonder
Nobles act on the stage. Below this level there's nothing.
Ah, but there is! The games! Go there for the ultimate scandal,
Looking at Gracchus who fights, but not with the arms of a swords-
 man,
Not with a dagger and shield (he hates and despises such weapons),
Nor does a helmet hide his face. What he holds is a trident,

What he hurls is a net, and he misses, of course, and we see him
Look up at the seats, then run for his life, all around the arena,
Easy for all to know and identify. Look at his tunic,
Golden cord and fringe, and that queer conspicuous armguard!
So the professional fighter who meets this kind of a Gracchus
Suffers the worst disgrace; a wound, at least, is an honor.

If the people could vote, and were free in their right of election,
How could they fail to choose a Seneca over a Nero?
More than one sack, one asp, one ape, one dog, would be needed
If his parricides earned the punishments due to their number.
Agamemnon's son, Orestes, murdered his mother.
That was a different case, with the gods giving orders for vengeance
Over a father slain while drunk. But even Orestes
Never polluted himself by cutting the throat of his sister,
Never murdered his wife nor poisoned cups for his cousins,
Never sang on the stage, nor attempted original epics!
Nothing in all the reign of this cruel and merciless tyrant,
Nothing he ever did was more deserving of vengeance.
Hail, our noble prince, and his works of art! What a leader,
Happy to pimp for the foreign stage, and with horrible singing
Earn the laurel wreath, or a Grecian garland of parsley!
Deck his ancestors' busts with the trophies won by his howling,
Place at Domitius' feet the sweeping gown of Thyestes,
Melanippa's mask, Antigone's robe; for a trophy
Hang the fiddle or harp high on the marble colossus.

Who had nobler sires than Catiline had, or Cethegus?
Yet here were two who planned attacks by night, burning houses,
Setting temples on fire, or hoping to. These were no Romans,

Sons, more likely, of Gauls from the West, the kind that wear
    breeches.
(What their garb should have been was the shirt, pitch-lined for the
    torture.)
But our consul, on guard, beat down their banners, a consul
Born of lowly blood, a man from humble Arpinum
Newly come to Rome, of equestrian rank, and he saved us
Setting his garrisons, armed, at every point in the city,
Watchful on every hill, while the frightened citizens trembled.
So, within our walls, a civilian, clad in a toga,
Gained renown as great as Octavian won at Philippi
Or the Actian shore, his sword blood-red from the battles.
Rome, a free Rome then, called Cicero Sire of His Country.
There was another man from that little town of Arpinum,
One who used to work for hire, in the hills of the Volscians,
Tired at the hales of another man's plough, and later a soldier
On whose pate, with a crash, came down the centurion's cudgel
If his shovel and pick were slow in the toil of the trenches.
This was the man, later on, who defended the terrified city
Facing the Teuton hordes and the heights of utter disaster.
So, when the ravens flew down, after the carnage was over—
Bodies as big as these were something new for their feasting—
Catulus, nobly born, had a share, to be sure, in the triumph,
But the real acclaim was for Marius, son of the people.
Decius the father, Decius the son, plebeians and heroes,
Offered themselves to the gods below, to the earth-mother goddess,
Vowing their lives to save the hosts of legions and allies,
All that Latin youth, and so made an offering, dearer
To their mother and gods than all the ranks of the rescued.

It was the son of a slave, the last good king of our seven,

Who won the robe and the rods, the diadem of Quirinus.
But the consul's sons were unbarring the gates of the city
For the tyrants' return from exile, acting like traitors
When they should have been bold, heroic for freedom,
Marvels of courage, inspired like Cloelia, swimming the Tiber,
The man at the bridge, or the man who put his hand in the embers.
It was a slave who revealed the secret plot to the senate
A slave who deserved to be mourned by the decent matrons in
     public,
While those evil sons took the scourge and the axes, and justice
Passed from the tyrant's whim to the lawful cause of the city.

It would be better, I think, if you sprang from the loins of Thersites
Then in your life went on to become an Achilles, and worthy
Of those arms Vulcan made; better so, than the other way round,
A son of Achilles in fact, but conducting yourself like Thersites.
You can go back a long way, tracing your roster of forebears,
Yet, in the end, you will find you came from a shameful asylum.
Your first ancestor, whoever he was, was a shepherd,
Or if not that, something worse, which perhaps I had better not
     mention.

On the griefs of a career man

NAEVOLUS, I want to know why you always look glum when you
    meet me,
Making an uglier face that Marsyas, flayed by Apollo.
Why does your face have the look that Ravola's had when they
    caught him,
The muff-diver, getting his beard all wet in Rhodope's you-know?
If a slave takes a lick at a tart, we always give him a licking.
You look more cast down than Pollio Crepereius,
The fellow who goes around prepared to pay triple interest
And never finds fools he can take. Why these wrinkles, all of a sud-
    den?
Surely you once were contented enough, a knight by indulgence,

The life of the party, whose wit had a sting, whose stories were
    naughty.
Now this is all in reverse: your looks are grim, and your head holds
A bush of dry hair, your complexion has lost what it used to be
    given,
The glow, the gleam, that came from the packs of hot Bruttian bird-
    lime.
Also, your legs are a mess, with the hair sprouting forth. What's the
    matter?
Why are you thin as a sick old man with the chills and the fever
Every fourth day? Could it be your symptoms are psychosomatic?
Sorrow and joy can affect the face as well as the spirit.
You seem to have changed your ways, to head in another direction.
Not long ago, I recall, you haunted the temple of Isis,
Ganymede's shrine in the temple of Peace, or Cybele's secret
Place on the Palatine Hill, or the fanes where Ceres was worshipped.
Any such temple, it seemed, was full of available women
For a coxswain like you, and though you said little about it,
If the supply was short, you could always make do with their hus-
    bands.

"This kind of life brings a profit to many; to me it brings nothing,
Maybe a greasy cloak to throw over my toga, some product
Off a Gallic loom, ill-woven, disgustingly colored,
Or maybe a little piece of silver, inferior metal.
The fates are the rulers of men, and the parts hidden under our gar-
    ments
Have their lot as well. Unless the stars are propitious,
Measurements out of this world—phenomenal!—prove to be useless
Even though Virro has seen us stripped and drools at the prospect,
Even though love letters come, continually coaxing and pleading.

What's that phrase from the Greek—*A man is drawn to a fairy*?
What in the world can be worse than the fairy who's stingy about it?
'Oh, but I paid you once, and I paid you twice, and I paid you
Ever so many times.' He's figured it out, or he hopes so,
Using every device. . . . Does he think this job is so easy,
Shoving it in to the point where it meets with yesterday's dinner?
Ploughing the master's field pays more than ploughing his person.
Ah, but he used to think himself such a delicate fellow,
Such a pretty boy, a Ganymede, worthy of Heaven,
Won't he ever be nice to his lowly pleasurers? Won't he
Ever be prepared to pay for his gratification?
Look at him! Isn't he sweet? We send him balls on his birthday,
Amber, I mean, for his hands to hold to keep them from sweating,
Or a green parasol, some humid day in the springtime,
Or, on the Matrons' Day, a lot of presents in secret
For him to dote upon as he lies in his chaise longue, beaming.
Tell me, you sparrow: for whom do you keep those Apulian moun-
    tains,
All those estates, those fields it tires the hawks to fly over?
You have storerooms filled with wines from Trifolian vineyards
Where the slopes look down on Cumae or Gaurus, deserted.
Who seals up more casks, and who is less likely to drain them?
Would it cost you so much to parcel out a few acres
To some client whose loins have been worn out in your service?
Why not bequeathe to me that little brat from the country
With his mother, their cottage, the puppy he likes to play with,
Rather than pass him on to your cymbal-walloping crony?
'Oh, you're not nice to ask,' says he. But who does the asking,
I, or the rent I must pay? I, or my single slave boy?
Single, yes, like the eye of Polyphemus the giant,
Single, but not for long; I shall have to purchase another,

Then both will have to be fed; and what shall I do in the winter
When the north wind howls, and their feet are cold, and they
    shiver?
What am I going to say—*Hold on, await the cicadas?*

"Well, suppose you do disavow some obligations,
What do you think this is worth, that unless you had me for a client,
Loyal, devoted, and true, your wife would still be a virgin?
Surely you know how often you asked for my help, and how many
Ways you suggested, how hard (excuse me!) you were in entreating.
So, more than once, when she fled your embrace, she was caught in
    another's,
Mine, whose else? when she'd broken her bonds, and was ready for
    signing
A contract with some other man. It took all night, but I saved her
While you wept outside. I appeal to the bed as a witness,
I appeal to you, who must have noticed its squeaking,
Not to mention her cries. Ah, many's the time when a marriage,
On the point of a break, is saved by a lover's arrival.
Why do you wiggle and shift? What's first, what's last, does it
    matter?
Ungrateful and treacherous man, is it nothing to you, is it nothing
That your little son and daughter descend from my kindness?
You bring them up as your own; you delight in putting on record
Names and dates that prove you a man. And so you're a father.
Hang up the wreaths on your door, for I have given you something
Counter to common talk. You have the rights of a parent.
You are entitled to be an inheritor in good standing,
With no discount to the state, and maybe a nice little windfall
All through my doing, and I can get you more if you say so.
Why not let me complete the tally, and give you three children?"

116

Naevolus, I must admit, you have just ground for complaining:
What does he say in reply?

                "He simply pays no attention,
Looks for another ass, the kind with two legs, for his pleasure.
Don't let this go any farther; it's all confidential, between us.
One of these pumice-smoothed boys is a deadly foe, if he hates you.
He is furious now, can't stand me for knowing his secrets,
Thinks I betray all I know. He'd readily take up a dagger,
Crack my skull with a blackjack, burn up my house with his torches.
Don't think him worthy of scorn, not altogether. The fact is
He can afford to pay any price if he wants to buy poison.
Keep all this to yourself, like the Council of Ares in Athens."

Ah, Corydon, Corydon, do you think a rich man can have secrets?
Maybe his slaves will keep still, but his asses will talk, and his hound-
    dogs,
His doorposts be tattletales, and even his columns of marble.
Shut the windows, pull the curtains, fasten the doors tight,
Douse the light, throw everyone out, let none sleep near by,
Still, what he does at the time the cock crows twice, by daylight,
Even before, will be known to the nearest innkeeper; also
He will have heard all the lies of his chief cooks and bottle washers.
That's the way they get even, a form of revenge for their beatings.
Some one will always be there, drunk at the crossroads, to find you,
Whether you like it or not, to bend your poor ear with his babble.
Those are the ones you should ask, instead of me, to be silent.
What a chance! They would rather have fun by betraying a secret
Than get stinking drunk on Falernian, sweeter if stolen,
Swilling at least as much as Saufeia conducting a service.
For a goodly life there are many excellent reasons,

But the greatest of these is to rise above servants' gossip.
The tongue is the slave's worst part. And yet, worse still is the master
Who cannot, or will not, be free of those whose spirits he nurtures
With his own money and bread.

                "Good advice, but a little too common.
What about my particular case, with so much time wasted,
Disappointment, dismay? For our life is most short and unhappy,
Fading away like a flower, and even while we are drinking,
Calling for garlands and girls and perfumes, old age steals upon us,
Always, before we know."

               Don't worry; there'll always be fairies
While these seven hills stand. They will come from all sides, some in
    wagons,
Some in boats, and you'll see them scratching their heads with one
    finger.
You have plenty to hope for; meanwhile, keep chewing your spear-
    mint.

"Tell this to luckier men. As for me, my fates are contented
If my belly can live on what my pecker provides it.
Poor little household gods, whom I invoke with a tiny
Pinch of incense or meal, or offer diminutive garlands,
When will I make a good shot to keep my old age from the poor-
    house?
I am not asking so much, a thousand dollars, plus interest,
Principal guaranteed, and a few little dishes of silver,
Not engraved, but the sort a Puritan censor would banish,
Also a couple of slaves, good husky Bulgarians, able
To carry me off at my whim to any seat in the Circus.

Then I'd like an engraver, a little stooped, and a painter
Who could quickly dash off any number of suitable portraits.
That would be all for a poor man like me, and more than sufficient.
What a pitiful prayer, and one I have really no hope of,
Since when Fortune is called on to do things for me, she is always
Stuffing her ears with wax from the ship that carried Ulysses
Safe past the Sirens' song, a luckier hero than I am."

On the vanity of human wishes

IN ALL the lands that reach from Gibraltar to the Euphrates
Few indeed are the men who can tell a curse from a blessing.
Few remove the mist of error—and when does our reason
Govern our hope or our fear? In your own case, what did you ever
Plan with the omens so good that you never thereafter repented
Making the try, or never repented the wish come true?
The gods are not difficult, really: all you need do is to ask them,
They would as soon as not bring down your household in ruins.
In peace, in war, in both, we ask for the things that will hurt us.
Many a man has found his flood of eloquence fatal,
Many have perished who trusted too much in the strength of their
    muscles,

Even more have been choked off by the money they hoarded,
By the estates whose expanse exceeded the normal condition
By as much as a whale from Britain surpasses a dolphin.
So, in the bad old days, because of the orders of Nero,
Longinus lost his home, and Seneca, grown too wealthy,
Saw his gardens placed under lock and key by the troopers.
Nero's orders, again, brought down on the Laterani
Vengeance and death, with a guard storming the gates of their palace.
There's one place that a soldier seldom invades; that's a garret.
If you are on the road by night, and carrying with you
Only an item or two of your less elaborate silver,
You fear a sword or a club or a reed that stirs in the moonlight,
But your poor man sings a song in the face of the robber.

Almost the first of prayers, best known in all of the temples,
Is the one for wealth: let riches increase, so our strongbox
May be the biggest in town. But aconite never is offered
Out of earthenware cups; the time to be fearful of poison
Comes when you reach for the goblet encrusted with jewels, when wine
Glows red in the bowl of gold. Praise, therefore, each of the sages,
The one who laughed and the one who wept, stepping over the threshold.
Easy, for any man, is the censure of merciless laughter.
Remarkable, though, that the eyes of the other one never ran dry.
Democritus used to shake his sides with contemptuous mirth
Though in the cities he knew there were no such things as our togas
Bordered or striped with the purple, palanquins, the fasces, tribunals.
What if he had seen the lofty car, with a praetor

Standing high as he rode through the dust and roar of the Circus,
Dressed in the tunic of Jove, with palms, and over his shoulder
A toga, Tyrian-dyed, with as many folds as a curtain?
Don't forget the crown, so heavy it can't be supported
By one single neck, but a sweating slave has to hold it
Riding beside his lord, in the selfsame car with his master.
(This serves to keep the consul from too much pride of position.)
Then there's the bird that springs from the ivory staff, and on one
    side
The blowers of horns, on the other the white-robed clients in long
    rows,
Whose dutiful friendship was won by the meal-ticket safe in their
    pockets.
Democritus, long ago, found ample occasion for laughter
No matter whom he met, and we can learn from his wisdom
That the greatest men, who set the greatest examples,
Sometimes are born in a land where the air is thick, and the people,
Muttonheads that they are, even thicker. He laughed at their trou-
    bles,
Laughed at their joys and tears, and if Fortune threatened, he told
    her,
Take a jump in the lake, and pointed the way with his finger.

Silly, or downright disastrous, are all the things that we pray for,
Weighting the knees of the gods with the words in the wax of our
    tablets.
Power and consequent envy hurl some men down to their ruin;
They are sunk by the long and illustrious list of their honors.
Their statues come down, they follow the rope, the axe cuts to pieces
The wheels of the car and the legs of the horses (who didn't deserve
    it).

Now the fires hiss hot—in the roar of bellows and furnace
Burns the head adored by the people. The mighty Sejanus
Makes a crackling sound, and out of that countenance, second,
Not so long ago, in the whole wide world, there are fashioned
Wine jars, frying pans, basins, and platters, and piss pots.
Laurel your doors and lead the great chalked bull to Jove's altar!
Sejanus gets the hook, he is dragged along. What a picture!
Everybody is glad. "Believe me, I never could stand him.
What a puss he had! But what were the charges against him?
Who were the witnesses, the informant? How did they prove it?"
"Nothing like that at all: the only thing was a letter,
Rather wordy and long; it came from Capri." "That's all right, then.
That's all I wanted to know."

                         And what are the people of Remus
Doing now? What they always do; they are following fortune,
Hating her victims, as always. Had Nortia favored Sejanus,
Had the leader's old age been unexpectedly stricken,
This same mob would have hailed as Augustus the man now
    doomed.
Ever since the time their votes were a drug on the market,
The people don't give a damn any more. Once they bestowed
Legions, the symbols of power, all things, but now they are cautious,
Playing it safe, and now there are only two things that they ask for,
Bread and the games.

                     "I hear that many are going to get it."
"Not a doubt in the world. They've got a big furnace all ready."
"Bruttidius looked a bit pale when I met him beside Mars' altar.
The beaten Ajax, I fear, suspects he's been poorly defended.
Now he'll get even for that." "All right, let's go, in a hurry—
While he lies on the bank, let's give Caesar's foeman a few kicks."
"Yes, and be sure the slaves can see, so that all must admit it.

We don't want to be dragged to court at the end of a halter."
That was how they talked, at the time, about their Sejanus.
That was the way the crowd muttered and grumbled about him.
So—would you like to have been Sejanus, popular, courted,
Having as much as he had, appointing men to high office,
Giving others command of the legions, renowned as protector
Of that Prince who's perched on the narrow ledges of Capri
With his Eastern seers and fortunetellers around him?
You would certainly like the spears, the horsemen, the cohorts,
The camp all your own. Why not? Even those with no craving for
     murder
Wish that they had the power. But what good would it be if it
     brought you
Risk in equal amount? Would you rather be robed like Sejanus,
Dragged along the streets like him, or would it be better
Taking charge of affairs in some little town like Fidenae,
Mayor of Gabii, or Inspector of Weights at Ulubrae?
So you acknowledge Sejanus did not know what to pray for,
Seeking excessive renown, excessive wealth, and preparing,
All the time, a tower whose stories soared to the heaven,
Whence he had farther to fall, a longer plunge to his ruin.
What was it overthrew the Crassuses, Pompeys, and that man
Under whose lash the people were made to bow in obeisance?
What brought them down? High rank, sought after with never a
     scruple,
And ambitious prayers, granted by gods who were evil.
Few are the kings who descend without wounds or murder to Pluto.
Few tyrants die a dry death.
                         As for your poor little scholar
Paying his penny tuition, with one slave guarding his schoolbag,
Even he begins to hope and to pray, in vacation,

For Demosthenes' fame, or Cicero's eloquent prowess.
Yet this talent of theirs brought both of them tumbling down,
Eloquence proving a flood, a torrent that overwhelmed them.
Cicero's head and hands were cut off through his genius for speak-
  ing.
No little stammerer's blood ever stained the rostra with crimson.
"Fortunate natal day for Rome, me being her consul":
If he had only spoken like that in all his orations,
He could have laughed to scorn the swords of Antony. Better
Write such ridiculous lines than the scathing Second Philippic.
Terrible, too, was the end of Demosthenes, marvel of Athens
For his power to arouse or control the moods of the people.
Under an evil star he was born, and the gods were against him
From the time he was sent from the forge, the coal, and the anvil
By his father, to learn the arts of the rhetorician.

All the spoils of war, the trophies fastened on tree trunks,
Breastplate, the strap that hangs from the broken helmet, the wagon
Whose yoke is cut off from its pole, the staff of a trireme con-
  quered,
A captive, depressed, on an arch of triumph—all these are consid-
  ered
Far above normal good things. To this height each general, Roman,
Greek, or barbarian, strains; for this he endures toil and danger,
Thirsting far more for renown than ever he thirsted for virtue.
Whose embrace would enfold Virtue without her rewards?
Yet, more often than once, a country has come to her ruin
Through the desire of a few, their lust for praise, for a title
That might cling to the stones that stand guard over their ashes,
Stones that the barren fig tree has crude enough vigor to shatter,
Seeing that even tombs have a day and a doom allotted.

Weigh out Hannibal's dust. How many pounds does he come to,
This greatest commander of all? Here was a leader, too mighty
Even for Africa's reach, from the Moorish sea to the desert,
From the steaming Nile to the elephant-teeming jungles.
Spain is under his sway, he leaps the Pyrenees mountains;
Nature bars his advance with the ice of the Alpine glaciers
But he splits the rocks with his vinegar, cracks mountains open,
Now he holds Italy, but still he intends to press onward.
"Nothing is won," he says, "until the soldiers of Carthage
Smash the gates of Rome and plant their flags in the forum."
What a face he had! What a wonderful theme for a picture,
A general with one eye riding an elephant—splendid!
What is the end? Alas for glory! He also is conquered,
Runs off to exile, and there, a truly magnificent client,
Sits in the court of a king, awaits his Bithynian pleasure.
What brought an end to the life that once confounded all nations?
Not a sword, not a stone, not a spear. The avenger of Cannae,
All those seas of blood, was a little ring that held poison.
Run, then, over the Alps, behave like an absolute madman,
To end up the schoolboys' delight, the theme of their declamations.

One world, so it seemed, was too little for Alexander.
That unfortunate youth raged at its borders—too narrow,
More confining than Gyara's rocks, or tiny Seriphos.
Yet when he came to the town with the walls of brick, he was happy
With a sarcophagus' bonds. Death, and death only, announces
What little things are the bodies of men. Herodotus tells us
How the ships once sailed through Mount Athos, with other inven-
    tions,
Not to say outright lies, of Greek historians, namely,
How that sea was paved with warships, turned into a highway

For the chariot wheels of Persia, and how, at his feasting,
Xerxes made rivers fail and drank up the streams in their courses.
Sostratus tells us the same, flapping damp pinions, or armpits.
The monarch who more than once had treated the winds to a flog-
ging,
Such as they never endured in the prison where Aeolus held them,
What kind of shape was he in, returning from Salamis, Xerxes,
Xerxes the king, who bound earth-shaking Poseidon in shackles,
Thinking himself no doubt very kind to have spared him a beating?
Which of the gods could serve this kind of master? But tell me
What kind of shape was he in coming back? With one single vessel,
Through blood-reddened waves, and the prow held back by the
corpses,
Such was his faring, the penalty paid for the glory he cherished.

"Give us many years, O Jupiter, give us long life!"
This is all you ask, in the bloom of health or in sickness.
But a long old age is full of continual evils:
Look, first of all, at the face, unshapely, foul, and disgusting,
Unlike its former self, a hide, not a skin, and chopfallen;
Look at the wrinkles too, like those which a mother baboon
Carves on her face in the dark shade of Numidian jungles.
Young people vary a lot; one, you will find, is more handsome,
One more robust, but the old are all alike, and they look it—
Doddering voices and limbs, bald heads, running noses, like chil-
dren's,
Munching their bread, poor old things, with gums that are utterly
toothless,
Such a disgusting sight to themselves, their wives, and their chil-
dren.
They are even despised by Cossus the legacy-hunter.

Wine is no good any more, food everlastingly tasteless.
As for the act of love, that long ago was forgotten,
Or if you should try, though you play with it all night long,
You will never rise, you cannot, to meet the occasion.
This is a state of things to pray for, this impotent sickness?
When desire outruns performance, who can be happy?

Now face up to the loss of another sense, that of hearing.
Who can delight in the song, however famous the singer,
Were it Seleucus himself at the harp, or the concord of players
Dressed in their golden robes? And to make it worse, it won't matter
Where your seat may be in the theatre; all of the brasses,
Blaring together, can scarcely be heard. If your slave wants to tell you
What time of day it is, or announce that a visitor's coming,
He has to bawl in your ear.
                                        And the blood gets thin in the body
Warmed by fever alone, and diseases, forming in column,
March and countermarch. If you ask me their names, I should find them
Harder by far to complete than the number of Oppia's lovers,
How many patients the doctor Themison killed in one autumn,
How many partners Basilus cheats, or how many pupils
Hamillus perverts in his school, how many wards Hirrus swindles,
How many men tall Maura exhausts in a day's occupation.
I could sooner add up the villas owned by the barber
I used to go to when young. One man is weak in the shoulder,
One's sacroiliac hurts; another suffers lumbago;
One has lost both eyes and envies the fellow with one left;
One's pale lips take morsels of food from another man's fingers;
One who used to open jaws wide at the sight of his dinner

Now can only gape like the chick of a swallow whose mother
Flies to fill his mouth. But worse than all bodily failings
Is the weakening mind which presently cannot remember
Names of slaves, nor the face of the friend he dined with last eve-
    ning,
Cannot remember the names of offspring begotten and reared,
So, by a cruel will, he disinherits his children,
Leaving his whole estate to a whore, for services rendered,
Such was the power of the breath of that mouth in the jail of that
    archway.
Perhaps he is strong of mind; even so, he must bury his children,
Gaze on the funeral pyre of the wife he loves, or his brother's,
Or the urns that hold the ashes and dust of a sister.
Such are the punishments paid to men who live long; they grow
    older
With the doom of the house renewed forever and ever.
Sorrow and grief abound, and the black raiment of mourning.
Nestor's life, if we place any trust in the stories of Homer,
Almost equalled the days of the long-lived raven. How happy
In that he put off his death through many a generation,
Counting his years beyond scores, drinking the new wine so often.
Happy? But wait just a moment—he found enough cause for com-
    plaining
Over fate's decrees, when he saw his Antilochus burning
On the funeral pyre, when he asked of every companion
Why he had lived so long, what crime he had done to deserve
    this.
So did Peleus mourn when he grieved for the loss of Achilles;
So did Laertes mourn over the sea-borne Odysseus.
Priam, perhaps, might have come to the shades while Troy was un-
    injured,

With Hector conducting the rites and the rest of his sons in at-
    tendance,
While Polyxena rent her robes, and Cassandra bewailed him,
If he had died at a different time, died long before Paris
Built the reckless ships that carried him seaward to Sparta.
What did his length of days bring him? The sight of his Asia
Overthrown, and the sword and the fire and the work of destruc-
    tion.
So he put off his crown, and, a trembling old man, but a soldier,
Fell like an agèd ox before high Jupiter's altar,
Giving his ancient throat to be cut by the knife of his master.
Such was Priam's fate, but at least his departure was human.
Hecuba ended her days as a yapping bitch by the seashore.

I come back to the men of our own race—never mind Croesus
Warned by the eloquent voice of Solon to look to his future.
Never mind the king of Pontus, astute Mithridates.
Look what a long life brought to Marius—exile and prison,
A life in the swamps of Minturnae, begging for bread in a city
Carthage, conquered by Rome. But now suppose he had fallen
Just as he stepped from his car, after parading his captives
With victorious pomp, triumphant over the Teutons,
Whom could Nature, or Rome, have blessed with a happier glory?
Looking ahead, the land of Campania offered to Pompey
A fever he should have preferred to the anxious prayers of the
    cities.
These restored him to health, but he was saved to be conquered.
Rome's good luck, and his own, spared his head for the sword of
    Achillas.
No such indignity came to Lentulus; Catiline's body
Fell in death, intact; and the same was true of Cethegus.

When a mother sees the shrine of Venus, she whispers
Modest prayers for her sons, and louder ones for her daughters,
Carrying fondness too far. "But why should you blame me?" she
    murmurs,
"Does not Latona rejoice in the beautiful form of Diana?"
All very well, but the rape of Lucretia forbids us to pray for
Any such beauty as hers, and Verginia would offer the hunchbacked
Rutila her good looks in exchange for her hump and her safety.
Any good-looking boy is a constant worry to parents.
All too rarely good looks combine with decent behavior.
Grant that an austere home has taught him its holy traditions,
Ways as noble and pure as those of the ancient Sabines,
Grant that beyond all this Nature has lavishly given
Continence, almost innate, and virtuous guise and expression—
(What better gifts can a youth receive from the kindness of Nature
Whose solicitous care has far more power than a guardian's?)—
Grant all this, and yet he will not be allowed to be manly.
His parents will sell him out; corruptors are daring, and lavish,
And money has absolute power. No autocrat in his castle
Ever castrated an ugly young man, no Nero would ever
Rape a club-footed boy, or one with the itch, or a hunchback.
Go ahead, if you like; rejoice in your young man's beauty.
So much the greater his danger. He will become a he-whore
Fearing the punishments the law allows cuckolded husbands.
No more lucky than Mars, the net will be spread for him also.
He will learn that sometimes a husband's rage is excessive,
Greater than law allows, the sword, or the lash, or the mullet.
But your pure young man will never be more than the lover
Of some matron he loves. You think so? You'll find that for money
He can perform without love, and strip her of more than her gar-
    ments.

What will she ever refuse, an Oppia or a Catulla,
Given a good wet lay? Between their legs is their conscience.
"What harm does beauty do if a boy is chaste?" What a question!
Go ask Bellerophon, go ask Hippolytus. Virtue
Did them no good at all with Stheneboea and Phaedra.
Hell hath no fury like a woman scorned, with her hatred
Lashed by her sexual rage.
                               And what advice should we give him,
That young man on whom the wife of Caesar is looking,
Eying with bigamous lust? The handsomest lad in the city,
The finest and best, patrician of birth, is a pitiful victim.
Messalina's eyes have doomed him to utter destruction.
She has been sitting there, with the bridal veil on her shoulders
While the bridal bed is spread in the public gardens,
While, with ancient pomp, the dowry, thousands on thousands,
Duly is paid with the seers and official witnesses present.
Do you think these are secret rites, known only to intimate cronies?
Never! A lady like this always gets legally married.
Tell him what to do now. Disobey her, and die before morning?
Or let her have her way, accept a reprieve, till the city
Hears of the whole affair and it reaches the ears of our leader?
The husband will be the last (they usually are) to suspect it.
Meanwhile, obey her commands, if a few days' life is important.
There is no such thing as an easier way, or a better.
Give your fair white neck to the sword—that much you can offer.

So—should men pray for nothing at all? If you're asking my counsel,
You will permit the gods themselves to make the decision
What is convenient to give, and what befits our estate.
We shall not get what we want, but the things most suitable for us.

Man is dearer to gods than he is to himself. We are foolish,
Led by blind desire, the spirit's extravagant impulse,
Asking for marriage and offspring, but the gods know what they'll
    be like,
Our wives and our sons. But still, just for the sake of the asking,
For the sake of something to give to the chapels, ritual entrails,
The consecrated meat of a little white pig, pray for one thing,
Pray for a healthy mind in a healthy body, a spirit
Unafraid of death, but reconciled to it, and able
To bear up, to endure whatever troubles afflict it,
Free from hate and desire, preferring Hercules' labors
To the cushions and loves and feasts of Sardanapallus.
I show you what you can give to yourself: only through virtue
Lies the certain road to a life that is blessed and tranquil.
If men had any sense, Fortune would not be a goddess.
We are the ones who make her so, and give her a place in the
    heavens.

With an invitation to dinner

ATTICUS, feasting in state, is considered a very *chic* fellow.
Rutilus, doing the same, is a madman. What do the people
Laugh at with louder guffaws than a poverty-stricken Apicius?
Every clubroom and bath, every bar, every theatre buzzes
Over Rutilus' case. He is active, young, and hot-blooded,
Not too old for the draft, but he seems to be out of control,
Signing up, or about to sign, with a trainer of gladiators.
Nobody makes him do this, but neither does any one stop him.
You will see many like him, with a frustrated creditor waiting,
Hoping perhaps he'll show up at the market to buy his provisions,
Since his only excuse for living lies in his palate.
On the verge of collapse, the wretch, for exactly that reason,

135

Feasts in extravagant style; no price is considered excessive
While he is trying to find something new in the way of *hors
    d'oeuvres*.
Matter of fact, the more it costs, the better he likes it.
It's no trouble at all to hock the family silver—
Ready cash is the stuff that seasons the plainest of dishes
Till, at the last, they come to the fare of gladiators.
So it matters a lot who it is that's providing the banquet.
Rutilus? What a waste! Ventidius? What a fine fellow,
Really a prince! It all depends on the state of his fortune.

I have no use for the man who knows how much higher Atlas
Is than the Libyan hills, and yet is unable to tell you
What the difference is between a purse and a strongbox.
Know thyself is worth keeping in mind, a watchword from Heaven,
Whether you look for a wife or covet a seat in the senate.
Thersites had better sense than to set up a claim for the armor
Worn by Achilles once, but hardly graced by Ulysses.
If you aspire to defend a difficult case, but important,
Give yourself some advice, find out first who you are,
An eloquent orator, really, or just a mouthpiece like Matho.
Take your own measure and keep it in mind, in great matters or
    small ones.
If you are buying a fish, don't go to the market for mullet
When all you have in your purse is the price of a sardine or minnow.
If your poke shrinks, but your gullet expands, what outcome awaits
    you
When your inherited goods and your own are devoured by a belly
Holding principal, interest, silverware, acres, and cattle?
The last thing such owners as these ever give up is the ring;
When his finger is naked, Pollio has to start begging.

Luxury need not look on early death as a terror;
What extravagance dreads is old age, more fearful than dying.

Here is the way it goes: they borrow money and blow it
Under the lender's nose, right here in the heart of Rome,
Then, when it's just about gone, and the creditor starts to turn
    pale,
They take it on the lam, run off to Baiae and oysters.
Leaving town is no worse, in their opinion, than moving
Out of a squalid slum to an air-conditioned apartment.
Only one thing breaks the heart of these *émigrés* leaving the coun-
    try,
That is missing the games and the Circus for one whole season.
They have lost the power of blushing, and only a few men
Fail to deride and jeer as decency flees from the city.

You will find out today, my good friend Persicus, whether
I live up, in my life, to all my beautiful maxims,
Whether I recommend beans, but live on *paté de foie gras*,
Whether I mean *petits fours* when I send my boy out for *polenta*.
Now that you've promised to come as my guest, you will find King
    Evander
Playing the part of your host; you can be the Tirynthian hero,
Hercules, or, if you like, the less important Aeneas,
Both with the blood of gods in their veins, both carried to Heaven,
One by water and one by fire.
                Now, Persicus, listen.
Here's what we're going to have, things we can't get in a market.
From a field I own near Tivoli—this you can count on—
The fattest kid in the flock, and the tenderest, one who has never
Learned about grass, nor dared to nibble the twigs of the willow,

With more milk in him than blood; and mountain asparagus gath-
ered
By my foreman's wife, after she's finished her weaving.
Then there will be fresh eggs, great big ones, warm from the nest
With straw wisps stuck to the shells, and we'll cook the chickens
that laid them.
We'll have grapes kept part of the year, but fresh as they were on
the vines,
Syrian bergamot pears, or the red ones from Segni in Latium;
In the same basket with these the fragrant sweet-smelling apples
Better than those from Picenum. Don't worry, they're perfectly
ripened,
Autumn's chill has matured their greenness, mellowed their juices.

Such a meal would have pleased our luxury-loving senate
In the good old days, when Curius, with his own hands,
Plucked from his little garden and brought to his little hearth-fire
Potherbs such as now your chain-gang digger of ditches
Turns up his dirty nose at, preferring the more familiar
Stink of sow's you-know-what in the reeking warmth of the cook-
shop.
In the old days, for a feast, they would have a side of salt pork
Hung from an open rack; for the relatives' birthdays, bacon,
Adding (perhaps) fresh meat, if a sacrificed victim supplied it.
To such a banquet would come a kinsman, thrice hailed as a consul,
One who had ruled over camps, invested with dictator's office,
Knocking off work for the day a little sooner than normal,
Over his shoulder the mattock with which he'd been taming the
hillsides.
When men trembled before the strictness of Cato the Censor,
Dreading the Fabii, Aemilius Scaurus, Fabricius

(For no censor believed himself safe from a colleague's rebuke),
No one, in those old days, thought it of any importance
What kind of tortoise shell swam in the waves of the ocean,
Destined to prop up the pates of our noblemen, Trojan-descended.
Couches used to be small, their sides unadorned, with a headpiece
Maybe of simple bronze, displaying the head of a burro
Crowned with leaves of the vine, a sight for the countryside bump-
      kins
To laugh at and caper around—everything perfectly simple,
Furniture, household, food.
                              Those were the days when the soldier,
Rough and tough, neither knew nor cared for the art of the Greeks.
After cities were taken, his share, perhaps, of the booty
Might have been goblets made by some magnificent artist.
So what?—he broke them up for trappings to put on his war
      horse,
To use for embossing his helmet and let his enemy, dying,
See the wolf made tame, as imperial destiny ordered,
Or the twins at the base of the rock, or the fearful sight of the War-
      god
Coming down with his spear and his shield. The silver of soldiers
Shone on their arms, nowhere else; they ate out of earthenware
      dishes.
Theirs were very fine ways, and more than deserving your envy,
If you can envy at all. The might of the temples was nearer:
The midnight voice was heard, and the gods themselves were their
      prophets,
Telling the heart of the town of the Gauls on their way from the
      ocean.
So we were solemnly warned, and Jupiter, made out of clay,
Undefiled by gold, proved that he cherished his people.

Those days saw our tables homemade from the native trees.
For such uses the wood was piled, if southeasterly gales
Brought the walnut down from its ancient hold on the hillside.
But your rich men now have no real pleasure in dining—
The fish and the game are insipid, the roses and perfumes stink,
If the citrus slabs don't rest on one ivory column
With a leopard's head at the top, the mouth wide open, and fash-
     ioned,
All of it, out of the tusks exported from Indian jungles,
From the Moroccan frontier, or some Arabian forest
Where the monstrous beasts had shed their fabulous weapons.
This is what gives a man good appetite, splendid digestion:
A silver table leg he scorns, like a ring made of iron.
Well, I avoid the guest, haughty and proud, who compares me
To himself (for the worse), and despises my humble appointments.
I have not even an ounce of ivory—look at my chessmen,
Look at my dice. My knives, you will notice, have handles of bone,
Yet I cannot see that the taste of my victuals is rancid,
Nor that the pullet I slice is any the worse for that reason.
I do not have any carver, to whom his whole school and profession
Have to bow down, the pride of Professor Tryphera, Doctor
Of courses instructing the boys how to cut up hares and sows' ud-
     ders,
Boars and springboks and pheasants, flamingoes, Gaetulian gazelles,
All very smart: *clack-clack*, blunt knives on the models of elm-wood
Till the whole quarter resounds. My own inexperienced youngster
Never learned in his life to snitch a guinea-hen's wing,
Help himself to a slice of venison; all that he ever
Managed to grab or gulp would be a morsel of cutlet.
As for my cups, nothing fancy, the kind you can pay for with pen-
     nies.

These will be handed around by a boy, no smooth type at all,
Dressed to keep himself warm, no Persian or Phrygian import
Bought from a dealer whose wares are entirely luxury items.
Any service you want you'll have to ask for in Latin.
All my boys dress alike; their hair is straight and close-cropped.
They have combed it today, but that's because of this party.
One is a sheepherder's son; the man who looks after the cattle
Fathered the other lad, who sighs when he thinks of his mother
Whom he's not seen for so long; he's more than a little bit homesick
For the cabin he knows and the four-legged kids that he plays with.
He has an honest look, natural, simple, and modest,
Such as those should have with the crimson stripe on their togas.
He doesn't go to the baths with an oil flask over his members,
Showing his armpits all shaved, an exhibitionist loudmouth.
He will serve you a wine that came from the very mountains
Where he was born himself, whose slopes he knew as his play-
    ground.
One and the same native land produced the wine and its server.

Possibly you may expect to watch the Ladies from Cadiz
Winning applause for their act, their song and dance, with the
    climax
When they sink to the floor and lie there bumping and grinding.
Brides enjoy watching this, with their husbands lying beside them,
Though it would be a disgrace to mention such acts in their pres-
    ence—
How, when desire is limp, the rich find means to arouse it.
Who can say which sex feels the more voluptuous pleasure?
The more it gets prolonged, for eyes and ears to delight in,
The greater the likelihood of wet pants, one way or another.
No such nonsense as this in my humble house. Let the rich man

141

Hear the clatter-bones, and the language too strong for the naked
Tart with the smelly groin; leave lust, and its arts and expressions
To the fellow who owns parquets of marble from Sparta
On which he spits out his wine. The rich deserve our forgiveness.
Men of moderate means are in disgrace if they gamble,
In disgrace if they wench, but the rich, doing this kind of business,
Merit our compliments: *gay souls, splendid fellows,* we call them.
In my house today there will be no such entertainment.
We shall read about Troy in Homer's epic or Virgil's
High and lofty song, so noble that what does it matter
Whose the voice that reads?
                                    Put away the cares of your business,
Give yourself a rest, the whole day long; never mention
Money at all; never mind if your wife goes out before daylight
Coming home at night with stigmata of irrigation,
With disheveled hair, and her face and her ears still burning.
Put aside your worries, and when you step over my threshold,
Think no more of your home, your slaves, and the damage they
    cause you
Breaking and losing things; forget your thankless companions.

Now the Great Games are on, and the praetor, seated in triumph,
Really becomes the prey of the horses, and, if I may say so
Without giving offense to the countless hordes of the people,
The Circus has captured Rome. The roar that beats on my eardrums
Tells me the Green has won; for you'd see the city in mourning
Otherwise, stricken dumb as after the battle of Cannae
When consuls lay low in the dust. These games are all right for the
    young,
With their noise and betting, the chance to sit with a girl at the
    races,

But let my wrinkled old skin soak up the sun in the springtime,
Giving the toga a miss. Here, though there's still a full hour
Till the sun is at noon, you can head for the bath, and no one will
    blame you.
Do this five days in a row, and you'll find yourself bored. Isn't pleas-
    ure
All the more keen in our lives the less we're inclined to repeat it?

On the near-shipwreck of a friend

THIS is a sweeter light, Corvinus, than my own birthday's.
Now the festal turf waits for its beasts, the ex-votos
I have promised the gods, a snowy lamb to Queen Juno,
One just as white for Minerva, whose breastplate is armed with the
 Gorgon,
And for Tarpeian Jove a victim who pulls the rope taut,
Tossing his head so the light keeps coming and going about him.
This is a fierce little bull, ripe for the temples and altar,
No more a suckling, but fit for pure wine poured over his forelock,
With his growing horns beginning to thrust at the oak trees.
If my fortunes at home were anything like my ambitions,
I would be dragging along a bull as fat as Hispulla,

Pliny's old aunt, a bull not nourished on neighborhood grasses,
But bulky and sluggish from cropping the rich green fields of Cli-
    tumnus,
Head held high and a neck no puny priestling should hack at—
This for my friend's return; he is trembling still, he has suffered
Horrible things, and now can hardly believe his own safety.
He has escaped the perils of sea, the blast of the lightning.
Dark and thick, the murk hid all the sky, and a flash,
Suddenly, out of one cloud, shattered the yardarms. Each man
Thought himself hit by the bolt, and in his terror was certain
No shipwreck ever was worse than this. The sails were on fire!
Everything happened here, the way it does in a poem,
Just that kind of a storm! And that wasn't all of it, either.
Listen, and pity again: there are many similar stories,
Terrible, widely known, as proved by the votive tablets
In our temples and shrines; does not Isis grant painters a living?

Just such a fortune as this was the lot of my good friend Catullus.
When the hold was half-drowned, and the vessel rolled in the bil-
    lows,
When the old gray-haired captain, for all his wisdom, seemed help-
    less,
While the mast wobbled and shook, he decided to jettison cargo.
This he learned from the beaver, who makes himself into a eunuch,
Willing enough to escape with the loss of his testicles, knowing
What a precious drug those glands produce by secretion.
"Heave my stuff overboard, every bit of it!" shouted Catullus,
Willing to fling to the winds even his finest possessions,
Purple garments fit for Maecenases, luxury lovers,
Other fabrics, dyed on the back of the sheep through the virtue
Of the generous grass, not to mention the marvelous water

(That must have helped, of course), and the Andalusian climate.
Also consigned to the deep went the silver plate and the salvers
Wrought in Parthenius' shop, the wine bowls worthy of Pholus
Holding three gallons apiece, the proper amount for Saufeia;
Also, baskets from Gaul, and dishes, up in the thousands,
Also, goblets, engraved, that Philip of Macedon drank from.
What other man in what part of the world would value his safety
More than his silver plate, or reckon his life above money?
Not for a living's sake do the greed-blinded try to make fortunes,
But their fortunes, it seems, afford the incentive for living.

Most of the cargo has gone, but the ship still wallows in danger.
There is a last resort, taking an axe to the mast,
A desperate measure indeed: save the ship by making it smaller.
Go now, trust your life to the winds, to a thickness of planking,
How many inches? Three, or six at the most, if you're lucky.
Next time you sail, take along not only your bags of provisions,
Your bread and your big-bellied flasks, but see you have plenty of
      hatchets.
Those you might need in a storm.
                                But the sea grew calm, and our sailor
Happened on better times, and his fate was stronger than ocean,
Stronger than wind, and the Sisters began to smile at their spinning,
Working with whiter strands, and a breeze whispered ever so gently,
Filling the shirts stretched out for sails and the one rag of canvas.
Then the wind died down, and hope came back with the sunshine.
Then the height appeared, Mount Alba, dear to Iulus,
More beloved by him than his stepmother's harbor, Lavinum.
This was the headland the Trojans named for the famous white sow
With the thirty young around her marvelous udders.

So Catullus comes to the moles that run like a bulwark
Out to enclose the sea, beyond the Tyrrhenian lighthouse,
Moles that meet again in the midst of the sea, with the mainland
Left far behind. This port is indeed an improvement on nature,
Wonderful to behold, and thither the captain is steering
With his crippled craft to the inner haven of safety
Where the frailest yacht could ride in peace, and the sailors,
Shaving their heads, as they vowed, babble about their adventures.

Go, then, boys, and with words and spirit attuned in devotion,
Garland the shrines, strew meal on the knives, adorn the soft altars
Made of green turf; I will follow, and, having performed my obla-
    tions,
Come again home, where my small images shine with the fragrant
Grace of the wax, to receive the verdant wreaths that adorn them.
Here I'll propitiate Jove, and offer the household Lares
Incense, and strew at their feet all bright-colored little flowers;
All things are shining here; the gateway rears its long branches,
The lanterns, ready since morning, are lit for the festal occasion.

Do not, I beg you, Corvinus, regard these rites with suspicion.
Catullus, for whose return I deck these altars, has children,
Three small heirs of his own. It would take you long to discover
Any one else who would give, for a friend who promises nothing,
One old sickly hen just closing her eyelids forever.
A hen would cost too much. Not even a quail will be offered
For a man with sons. But if the wealthy Galitta,
Or if Pacius, rich too, feel the least touch of a fever,
Every pillar along their porches will blossom with tablets
Hung in due form, and men will come out, the hecatomb-vowers,

Promising oxen by hundreds, since elephants cannot be purchased
Here in our land, but are brought from the darkest African jungles
To feed in Rutulian woods and the ancient meadows of Turnus.
The emperor owns the herd; they will bow to no private master
Since their ancestors took orders from Hannibal, Pyrrhus,
Roman generals, too, and their backs would carry whole cohorts—
No mean part of the war!—in the howdahs they bore into battle,
Novius would not delay, nor Pacuvius from the Danube
Hesitate at all to bring such an ivory creature
As offering to the shrine, a victim for Gallitta's Lares.
None more worthy of such great gods nor their reverent seekers.
Either of these, should you grant him permission, would willingly
offer,
Willingly vow, to the shrine the handsomest one of his slave boys,
Decking them out, and his maidservants too, with the ritual fil-
lets.
Or if he had in his house a daughter like Iphigenia,
Of an age to be wed, he would lead her up to the altar,
Though he could hardly expect the deer of the tragic poets
To be put in her place, a stealthy kind of replacement.

I have to give him praise, my fellow citizen; never
Do I think of comparing a thousand ships to a will;
If the sick man escapes the goddess of death, he's a goner,
Caught in another net; he will tear up his will, write a new one
Making Pacuvius heir, for splendid services rendered,
Not only heir, but sole heir: one stroke of the stylus will do it.
Won't Pacuvius go walking tall, with his rivals confounded!
So you can see how worth while was that wonderful deal at My-
cenae,

Cutting a maiden's throat. Long live Pacuvius! Let him
Have as many years as Nestor, and have as much money
As Nero ever stole, pile gold as high as a mountain.
Let him love no man, and let no man ever love him.

For a defrauded friend

ANY performance that sets an evil example displeases
Even its author himself: to begin with, punishment lies
In the fact that no man, if guilty, is ever acquitted
With himself as judge, though he may have won in the courtroom
Bribing the praetor in charge, or stuffing the urn with false ballots.
How do you think all men are feeling, Calvinus, about
Your charge of breach of trust, this latest criminal action?
But you are pretty well off, you'll not be sunk by such losses,
You're not the only one; this kind of case is familiar,
Not to say trite, one grain from the piled-up anthill of fortune.
Let's cut out the excessive laments. A man's indignation
Ought not burn out of bounds, nor be bigger than his wound is.

You, on the other hand, can hardly endure an iota,
The littlest least of light loss, and your bowels are all in an uproar
Simply because a friend declines to return you a sacred
Trust, committed to him. But does this really surprise you,
A man of your age, sixty years, born when Fonteius was consul?
Has not, in all this time, experience taught you better?

Great, to be sure, is Wisdom, who gives us her holy scripture:
Fortune bows down to her, but we also consider as happy
Those whom life has taught to put up with discomforts and nuis-
    ance
Without tossing the yoke. What day is ever so festal
That it fails to produce a thief, a swindler, a traitor,
Profits made out of crime (all sorts), and money won by the dagger,
Won by the poisoned cup? There are few good men, not as many
As the gates of Thebes, or the mouths of the Nile. We are living
In the ninth age of the world, more base than the era of iron.
Nature finds no name for this wickedness, having no metal
Fit to call it by, no alloy like its corruption.
We invoke the faith of gods and men with a clamor
Loud as free handouts earn Faesidius when he's orating.
Tell me, old boy (I say *boy*, because you ought to be wearing
Phylacteries round your neck, the badge of your second childhood),
Tell me, don't you know the allurements of other men's money?
Don't you know that the mob laughs at your simple behavior
When you insist that a man, any man in the world, should be truth-
    ful,
Never perjure himself, but believe in divinity's presence
Where the temples rise and the altars are colored with crimson?
Once upon a time men lived this way, in the old days,
Long before Saturn took up the sickle instead of the scepter,

With Juno a cute little girl, and Jove, in the caverns of Ida
Sequestered, not even a prince. Not yet did the dwellers in Heaven
Banquet above the clouds, with Hebe and Ganymede
Bringing the cups; not yet did Vulcan swig down his nectar,
Wipe off his sweaty arms black from Aeolian anvils.
Each god used to dine by himself, no such rabble of idols
As there is today, and the stars were content with a smaller
Roster of heavenly powers, a lesser load for poor Atlas.
No one had drawn by lot the gloomy underworld empire;
There was no glowering Dis beside his Sicilian consort,
There was no wheel, no rack, no black and punishing vulture,
There were no Furies at all, but the Shades, without any monarchs
In the realms below, were quite contented and happy.
Lack of probity then was something truly surprising,
A terrible sin, they thought, and worthy of death, if a young man
Did not rise and stand to show his regard for his elders.
Any bearded man, no matter who, was entitled
To a boy's respect, though the latter's home might be richer,
With more strawberries there, and huger mountains of acorns.
Reverence came to the man who was older, if only by four years.
Was the first down of youth equal to honored old age?

But today, if a friend does not deny that you gave him
Money to keep in trust, if he gives back the old leather wallet
With the rusty coins, what a portent we call it! Prodigious!
Garland and slaughter a lamb! Make it a matter of record!
If I see a man of integrity, what an occasion!
Really a freak, I would say, like a boy with a double member,
Like fishes found under a plough while the wide-eyed yokel marvels,
Like a pregnant mule, like a rain of stones. This upsets me
As would a cluster of bees if it swarmed on the roof of a temple,

As would a river that poured torrents of milk to the ocean.

You have been robbed, you complain, of something like five hun-
    dred dollars—
A swindle, a sacrilege! But what if another man's losses
Equal ten thousand? what if still another has lost even more,
So much more, in fact, that a strongbox could never contain it?
It's simple, it's easy enough, if no mortal man knows about it,
For the thief to scorn or despise the gods who are watching from
    Heaven.
Hear his loud voice as he lies! Look at his brazen expression!
By the rays of the Sun (he swears), by Jupiter's lightning,
By the spear of Mars, the darts of Apollo of Delphi,
By Diana's quiver, by the trident of Aegean Neptune,
Then, for good measure, he adds Hercules' bow and Minerva's
Lance and anything else in the ordnance supply-rooms of Heaven.
If he's a father, he adds, with tears, "May I eat for my dinner
The boiled head of my son with Egyptian vinegar dressing,
If I'm not telling the truth!"

Some men think that luck determines everything mortal,
Nobody governs the world, but Nature revolves in their courses
The changes of day and of year; and men like these, without awe,
Touch any altars you please. Another type always is fearful
Punishment follows crime, he thinks there are gods, but no matter,
He perjures himself just the same. "Let Isis decide what she pleases
With this body of mine, let her shatter my sight with her sistrum,
Just so, in blindness, I keep the coins I deny I have stolen;
Ulcers that bleed, or one lung, or half a leg—these are worth it.
If Lados, the champion runner, were poor, but still had his senses,
Needing no hellebore cure, no psychotherapist's counsel,

He should not hesitate to pray for the rich man's ailment
Known as the gout: what good is speed, the renown of a sprinter?
Can you make a meal on a branch of Olympian olive?
Maybe the wrath of the gods is great, but it's certainly tardy.
If they take the pains to punish all of the guilty,
When will they get to me? And I might find the god can be prayed
    to,
Pardoning deeds like mine. The fates of criminals differ.
One gets the cross, another the crown, for the same misdemeanor."

So he consoles his mind for his guilt and trembles in terror.
Call him to purge himself at the shrine, and he'll get there before
    you,
Ready to drag you there, to worry and nag you to test him.
Nothing like nerve and gall to make a bad case look better;
Boldness induces belief. He brazens it out, like the comic
Runaway clown in the play composed by the clever Catullus.
All you can do, poor dupe, is to bellow louder than Stentor,
Louder than Homer's Mars: "Do you hear this, Jupiter? Do you
Not so much as move your lips, when you ought to be vocal,
Marble though you may be, or bronze? Then why are we placing
On your burning coals the packets of holy incense,
Calves' liver, white hog-caul? As far as I can discover,
There's no choice to be made between your images, graven,
And Vagellius' bust."

                    And now, for your consolation,
Hear what a man can say who is neither a Cynic nor Stoic,
(They don't differ much more than a tunic's thickness would meas-
    ure),
A man who holds no brief for Epicurean contentment

With the growing slips in one diminutive garden.
Puzzling cases should be referred to the best of physicians,
But yours could be diagnosed by a chiropractor's apprentice.
If you can show me no deed in the whole wide world as disgusting
As what happened to you, I'll have nothing to say, I'll not tell you
To leave off thumping your chest with your fists, or pounding your
       cheeks
With the flat of your palm. Since ruin has been accepted,
The doors of the house must be closed, and the weeping and wailing
       be louder
Than they would be for a death. The loss of money is awful,
Such a terrible thing that no one can counterfeit mourning,
No one be content with merely rending his garments,
Rubbing his eyes to produce crocodile tears. If your money
Is gone, you will really cry with genuine lamentation.

But if you see all the courts filled up with complaints like your own,
If the tablets are read, inspected, turned over and over,
Then are pronounced a fraud, mere wood and wax, or waste paper,
In spite of the handwriting there, or the print of the sardonyx seal-
       ring,
Kept in its ivory case, alas! my dear fellow, Calvinus,
Do you think this makes you unique, some kind of a white hen's
       chicken,
The rest of us all common fowl, hatched out of eggs ill-omened?
You have not lost very much, you could bear this with moderate
       choler
If you would turn your eyes toward greater crimes. Take, for instance,
The hired hoodlum, the fire lit by the arsonist's sulphur
Burning the gates of your house; or think of those robbers of temples
Taking off great cups whose very rust should be worshipped,

The gifts of the people, or crowns, the oblations of ancient mon-
 archs.
If these are not there, a lesser profaner arises
To shave the gilded face of Neptune, or Hercules' thigh,
To strip the gold leaf off Castor. Why not? But the thief prefers
 bigger
Game, the melting down of Jupiter, Lord of the Thunder.
Or consider, again, the makers and merchants of poison,
The parricide thrown to the sea in the hide of an ox, and beside
 him,
Since the fates are adverse, an entirely innocent monkey.
This is only a part of the criminal calendar, running,
Daily, from dawn to dark: if you're eager to learn the behavior
Of the human race, this courthouse should more than suffice you.
Spend a few days there, and when you come out, you will hardly
Dare call yourself out of luck. Would a goiter surprise anybody
If it appeared in the Alps? Would a tourist in upper Egypt
Marvel that bubbies there were bigger than big fat babies?
Who is stunned at the sight of a blond-haired, blue-eyed German
Making horns of his hair, with ringlets moistened and twisted?
This is the way things are, and all share a common nature.
A pygmy runs to the wars in his diminutive armor,
Facing the Thracian cranes, their resonant clouds and their swoop-
 ing,
Soon to be caught, overmatched, by his enemy, and swept upward,
Borne in crooked claws through the curving air. If you saw this
Here in Rome, you would laugh yourself sick; but there, where the
 cohorts
Tower twelve inches high, at these continuous battles
Nobody ever guffaws.

     "Shall he go scot free, then, this traitor,
Swindler, perjurer, crook?" Well, now, suppose he is hustled
Off in the heaviest chains, or—what more could your anger be asking?—
You still don't recover your money,
Put to death at our whim. You still don't recover your money,
You don't get any refund. "But the least drop of blood from the
  headless
Body will give me some comfort, a solace to mix with my hatred.
Vengeance is sweeter than life!" That's how the ignorant babble,
Those whose hearts you see on fire for the slightest of reasons
Or for no reason at all. But you will not hear a Chrysippus
Talking like this, you won't hear the gentle genius of Thales
Making any such sounds, and the old man who lived near Hymettus,
The honeysweet mountain, would not have forced on his cruel accuser
  cuser
So much as one drop of the hemlock he had to drink in his dungeon.
Wisdom, by slow degrees, strips off our vices and follies,
Teaching us what is right. For Vengeance always is silly,
The proof of a mean little mind, and here is one way you can tell it:
No one enjoys revenge nearly so much as a woman.

But why should you think they have gotten away with their crimes,
  when awareness
Of their evil deeds holds their minds in bemusement,
Lashing with strokes unheard, and the soul supplies its own torture
Wielding the secret whip? A terrible punishment, truly,
Far more savage than those of Caedicius or Rhadamanthus,
To carry in one's own heart, by night, by day, his accuser.
Once upon a time a Spartan was told by the priestess
Of the Pythian shrine that punishment surely awaited
Any man who planned, as he did, to hold on to the money

Placed in his trust, and then compound the offense by false witness.
He was asking, it seems, what was the mind of Apollo,
Whether the god would approve or sanction any such project.
So he gave it all back, because he was frightened, not honest,
Nevertheless, in the end, he found that the voice from the temple
Told the reverend truth, for, with his sons and his household,
With relations far removed from immediate kinship,
He was destroyed. The mere wish to sin brings on retribution.
He who plots a crime, though it never is openly mentioned,
Has the guilt of the deed.
                              Suppose he succeeds in his purpose.
He is forever obsessed by anxiety, even at dinner.
His jaws are as dry as if he were sick; his bread he can't swallow,
Can't even chew, poor wretch, and he spits out his wine on the floor,
Finding the precious old Alban vintage completely distasteful.
Show him a better wine, and he starts to wrinkle his forehead,
Making a face as wry as if it had come from Falernum,
Vinegar, sourer than swill. In the night, if his worry permits him
Even the briefest rest, and his tossing limbs become quiet,
In his dreams he sees, straightway, the temple, the altar
Of the outraged god, and, even more of a burden
On his night-sweating soul, he sees you, looming above him,
Larger than life, a threat, a menace, exacting confession.
Such men tremble and pale at every flash of the lightning;
When it thunders, they swoon at the very first rumble from heaven,
Not as if it were chance, or the madness of winds, but that fire
Falls on earth in wrath, vindictive deliberate judgment.
That storm did no harm, but the next is all the more frightful
For the illusion of calm, the false postponement of vengeance.
If they begin to ache with pains in the side, and a fever,
They are certain the god has sent this illness upon them,

These are the stones he hurls, these are his lances and arrows.
They dare not vow to his shrine a bleating victim, nor offer
The Lares a crested cock; the guilty sick are not granted
Hope: what victim is not more entitled to living than they are?
The nature of evil men is mostly capricious and shifty.
When they commit a crime, they have more than enough resolu-
    tion,
But the sense of right and wrong—that seems to come to them only
After the deed is done. Still, habit becomes second nature—
Back to the scene of the crime. Who ever places a limit
On his own season of evil? When does he ever recover
The blush that has been expelled in disgrace from the hardened
    forehead?
Whom have you ever seen content with one villainous action?
Sooner or later this rascal of ours will get into trouble,
Step in the noose, succumb to the hook of the dungeon in darkness,
Face the Aegean rock, the cliffs and crags that are crowded
With our illustrious exiles. You will rejoice that a bitter
Punishment comes to the name you hate, and you will be happy,
At long last, and admit that the gods have all of their senses,
That not one is deaf, or blind like Tiresias the prophet.

On education in avarice

THERE are a great many things, Fuscinus, of evil renown,
Things that are bound to stain and sully the brightest of fortunes,
Taught and handed down to the sons of a house by the fathers.
If the old man throws dice and loses, the son has to gamble
While he is still in his teens, and rattles his own little dicebox.
Nor need relations hope for better things from that youngster,
Who, with a gourmand sire, a hoary old glutton as teacher,
Knows all about peeling truffles, all about seasoning mushrooms,
All about drowning in gravy the delicate beccaficoes.
When he's not much more than seven years old, still losing his milk
    teeth,
You could place on each side a thousand reverend masters,

Bearded and grave, but his appetite still would be for the dainties,
For the sumptuous style, for the most fastidious tables.

Does Rutilus teach us to show a merciful disposition,
Charity toward slight faults? Does he think that body and spirit
Are made of the selfsame stuff in the case of slaves and of freemen?
Or does he teach us to rage, to rejoice, as he does, in the cruel
Sound of the whip, a music more sweet to him than the Sirens'?
A tyrant of giant size he is to his trembling household,
Happy only at times when he summons the torturer, branding
Some poor slave with hot iron for snitching a couple of towels.
What is a young man taught by a sire who delights in the clanking
Of the iron chains, the branded slaves, and the dungeons?
Are you greenhorn enough to suppose that the daughter of Larga
Won't grow up to be a promiscuous bitch, when it took her
Thirty deep breaths, as a child, to get through the list of the lovers
Known to sleep with her mother? Even when she was a virgin,
Mamma would tell her all; and now, at Mamma's dictation,
She fills little wax tablets, and sends them off to her lovers
By the very same queers. Such is the order of Nature.
Evil examples at home corrupt us all the more quickly
Since they subvert our minds with the sanction of loftier warrant.
Maybe one youth, or two, might possibly scorn this behavior,
Souls made of better clay by the kindlier art of the Titan.
As for the rest, they are led in the evil paths of their fathers,
Dragged in the wheel-ruts of guilt shown to them over and over.

So, shun damnable deeds. For this there's at least one good reason—
Lest our children repeat the crimes we have taught them. We all
Are easily led, too prone to imitate wicked behavior.
Catilines can be found in all kinds of people and places,

But a Brutus is rare, and a Brutus's uncle is rarer.
Let no dirty word or sight step over the threshold
Where a father dwells. Far off, far off, ye unholy
Girls who work for pimps, parasitical night-wasting singers!
To a child is due the greatest respect: in whatever
Nastiness you prepare, don't despise the years of your children,
But let your infant son dissuade you from being a sinner,
For if, in days to come, he earns the wrath of the censor,
Being a man like you not only in body and features,
But also the son of your ways, a walker in all of your footsteps,
Treading deeper in vice, you will—oh, of course!—be indignant,
Rail with bitter noise, and make a new will. That will teach him.
Yet what makes you assume the father's frown, and the father's
Freedom of speech and act, when you behave worse, as an old man,
Than he ever did, and the windy cupping-glass searches
Vainly around your head for brains that it cannot discover?

When a guest is to come, none of your household is idle.
"Sweep the floor, polish the columns, get the spiderwebs down from
    the ceiling,
One of you clean the plain silver, another the embossed pieces."
That's their master's voice, and his whip is ready and waiting.
So the poor fool has the shakes lest his visitor's eyes be offended
By a dog-turd in the hall, or a portico spattered with mud,
Things that one little slave could clean up with a bucket of sawdust,
Yet he takes no pains that his son may see the house always
Free of guilt and stain. It is splendid to give to your country,
To give to your fellow men a citizen, if you can make him
Valuable to the state, a servant useful, devoted
Both in the wars and the acts required by peace. It will surely
Make all the difference, in what arts and habits you train him.

The stork feeds her chicks on snakes and on lizards found in the
      brambles,
Such will be the prey of the young when they're fledglings no longer;
The vulture brings to her brood carrion sought from the gibbet,
From dead cattle and dogs, and this is the food of the vulture
When he becomes full-grown and builds his own nest in the treetop.
But the eagles of Jove prey on the rabbit or roebuck
In the upland heights, and bring this fare to their eyries,
So when the eaglets mature, they seek for that prey, in their hunger,
Which they tasted first, soon after the eggshells were broken.

Cretonius likes to build houses: now on the bay of Caieta,
Now on Tivoli's height, now on Praeneste, his mansions
Rise with marble brought from Greece or lands beyond Ocean,
Overtopping the shrines of Fortune or Hercules, even
More than Posides the eunuch surpassed our Capitol building.
While Cretonius lived in houses like these, he diminished
Much of his fortune, he spent his wealth, but hung on to a portion
Not by any means small, but his son, a madman, destroyed it
Rearing still newer homes, with marble even more costly.

Those whose lot it was that their fathers worshipped the Sabbath
Pray to nothing now but the clouds and a spirit in Heaven;
Since their fathers abstained from pork, they'd be cannibals sooner
Than violate that taboo. Circumcised, not as the Gentiles,
They despise Roman law, but learn and observe and revere
Israel's code, and all from the sacred volume of Moses
Where the way is not shown to any but true believers,
Where the uncircumcised are never led to the fountain.
Remember the Sabbath Day, to keep it lazy. The father,
Setting this day apart from life, is the cause and the culprit.

Young men need not be taught to imitate most of the vices,
Only avarice seems to oppose their natural instinct.
Here is a vice, for once, in the shape and shade of a virtue,
Gloomy of mien, and dour indeed in dress and expression.
The miserly man is praised, of course, as if he were frugal,
A saving soul, to be sure, a craftier keeper of fortunes
Than the dragon of Pontus or the Hesperidean gardens.
Add the fact that the people thinks of the man whom I mention
As an artist at gain: estates increase with such forge-men
And they increase every way, becoming bigger and bigger.
The anvil is never still and the furnace forever is blazing.

So when a father thinks that the avaricious are happy,
Looks openmouthed at wealth, and figures no poor man is blessed,
He is urging young men to follow along that highway,
To study in that same school. There are A B C's of the vices;
These he indoctrinates first, compelling his pupils to master
The meanest, the pettiest things, but before too long he instructs
    them
In the insatiable hopes and passions for acquisition.
He cramps the guts of his slaves with the shortest, most meager, of
    rations
While he is starving himself, for he cannot possibly manage
To eat up the pieces of bread, the mouldy blue-colored remnants.
Even in middle September, the hottest, unhealthiest season,
Yesterday's mincemeat he saves, and saves, for tomorrow's dinner,
Beans and half an old fish, a stinking mullet or rock cod,
Counting the sections of leek he slices to put away with them.
Bidden to such a feast, a beggar from one of the bridges
Surely would send his regrets. But why accumulate riches

Through such tortures as these, when it seems the most obvious
    madness
Living the life of a tramp, to be a rich man on your deathbed?
Meanwhile the moneybag swells, grows fat, and in just that propor-
    tion
The love of money bloats up, and he who has only a little
Covets it least. As for you, a single house in the country
Does not suffice at all, you will have to purchase another,
Have to extend your acres, because the neighboring cornfield
Seems both bigger and better, so you buy it up, and the woodland,
Also the slope of the hill thick with the gray-green olive.
If the owner declines to sell under any conditions,
You can send over by night lean oxen, famishing cattle,
Into the green of his fields, and tired though they are, they will never
Find their way home till they've stored the whole crop in their rav-
    enous bellies,
So that you well might believe it was mown by close-cropping
    sickles.
You could hardly say how many men are bewailing
Wrongs like these, nor how many fields are sold by such tactics.

But how people do talk! What a blast from the trumpets of rumor!
"What's the harm?" says he, "I'll take the pods of my lupine
Over a neighborhood's praise, not to mention the district's,
If it means that I reap the scanty crops of a small farm."
Doubtless you will be free of the grip of diseases and weakness,
You will escape grief and care, and the days of your life will be
    longer,
Blessed with a happier fate, if all by yourself you are owner
Of as much tilled land as the whole Roman people together
Ploughed when Tatius was king. Later, to broken old Romans

Hurt in the Punic Wars, or the battles with terrible Pyrrhus
Or the Molossian swords, hardly two acres were given,
A bonus for countless wounds. Yet no one thought it was meager,
A miserly recompense for their service of tears and bloodshed;
No one said that the land was niggardly, thankless, ungrateful.
One little plot such as this was more than enough for the father
And the folk of his house, a pregnant wife, and four children
Playing around the yard, three of them free, one a slave child.
There'd be another meal steaming, gigantic kettles of porridge,
When their big brothers came back from working at ditch or at
     furrow.
Any such area now does not suffice for our gardens.

Hence come the causes of crime: there is no greater incentive
Toward compounding of poisons or thickening blows with the dag-
     ger
Than the desire of wealth beyond all moderate limits.
Get rich, get rich quick. But how can a desperate miser,
Hustling for all he's worth, ever expect to develop
Fear or respect for the law, or a decent sense of proportion?
"Live content, my sons, with your hills and your little cabins,"
That's what a Marican father might say, or a Vestine old-timer,
"Let's win our bread by the plough, enough and no more for our
     table;
This our country gods praise, whose help and goodness have given
The blessing of wheat instead of the hated old diet of acorns.
A man who is not ashamed to wear hip boots when it's icy,
Turning away the cold with reversible furs, you will never
Find him wanting to do actions he knows are forbidden.
It's the purple garb, the raiment peculiar and foreign,
Whatever it may be, that leads us to wicked behavior."

Those were the maxims the ancients gave to their children, but
 these days,
After autumn's end, a father at midnight awakens
A son who's asleep on his back and yells at him, "Wake up, get
 going,
Pick up your tablets and write, read up on your cases, and study
The red-lettered laws of the past, or seek the centurion's office.
See that Laelius notes your head, untouched by the comb,
Your hairy nostrils, and stares at your great big masculine shoulders.
Sack the huts of the Moors, the forts of the brigands of Britain,
So that your sixtieth year will bring you the wealth-giving eagle,
Or, if you're lazy and think the rigors of service too tiresome,
If your bowels move at the sound of horn or of trumpet,
Try to find something to sell for a profit, say fifty per centum;
Don't turn up your nose at a business that has to be banished
To the far side of the Tiber, and don't make any distinction
Between the odor of hides and attar of roses; a profit
Always smells good, no matter what possible source it may come
 from.
Here is the slogan for you, a maxim worthy of poets,
Even if Jove himself turned bard: *No one asks where you get it,*
But money is what you must have." These are the lessons for tod-
 dlers
Taught them before they can walk by dried-up haggard old nurse-
 maids,
This the girls all learn before their Alpha and Beta.

If a father insists on imparting such admonitions
I would speak to him thus: "Tell me, you silly old codger,
Who is giving the orders to hurry so fast? I would bet you
The pupil will master the teacher. Give up. Go away. Take it easy.

You will be beaten as surely as Telamon was by his Ajax,
As Peleus was by Achilles; don't be too stern with the youngsters.
Their marrowbones are not yet filled with the ripeness of evil.
When he begins to submit the length of his beard to the razor,
He will be a false witness, a perjury peddler, a cheap one
Touching the altar and foot of the goddess Ceres in swearing.
Have you a daughter-in-law? She's as good as dead if she carries
A dowry over the threshold. Whose fingers will throttle her sleeping?
Things that you think should accrue by land and by sea, he will figure,
Come his way by a shorter road; a great crime is no trouble.
"I never taught him those ways, I never gave him such precepts!"
Maybe not, in words; but you are the source and the fountain
Of his evil intent, for any father who teaches
Love of great wealth and inspires greed in his sons by the warnings
Given in sinister ways, who shows him how he can double
Patrimony by fraud, gives him a license, free rein,
Absolute control: if you call him back, you'll not stop him
Once he is under way. He'll laugh at you in derision
As he rushes along, with the point of return far behind him.
No one believes it's enough to be a partial delinquent,
So far, no farther! Oh, no—they give themselves license much greater.

When you tell a young man he's a fool to give a friend presents,
To help a relation in trouble, to lighten his poverty's burden,
You teach him to rob and to swindle, to use any criminal method
That will help him get rich. Your own devotion to money
Is as great as the Decii had for their country, as great as
Menoeceus held for Thebes, if the Greeks bear reliable witness,

Thebes, where the legions sprang from the dragon's teeth in the
   furrows,
Warriors born with shields, and joining in terrible battle
Just as if in their midst a bugler had instantly risen.
So you will see the fire, whose sparks you have struck, burning
   widely,
Carrying everything off. You will not be spared either, poor trembler.
The lion you taught will roar loud in his den as he mangles his
   master.
Your horoscope may be known to astrologers. Surely. But waiting
Takes a long time, and the thread is better cut off than spun out.
You stand around in his way, delay his prayers of thanksgiving.
Your enduring old age is a young man's horrible torment.
Quick! Send for Archigenes, or purchase some of the compounds
Mithridates has mixed. If you want more fruit from the fig tree,
If you want to gather ye roses, you'd better, before you have dinner,
Down the prescription devised by a king who was also a father.

I show you a splendid attraction, one you can't possibly equal
On the stage or at games supplied by the smartest of praetors,
If you will only watch at what peril to life the possessions
Of men's fortunes increase, or the treasure grows in the strongbox,
Or, more and more, the coins are banked in the temple of Castor
Since that day when Mars the Avenger was robbed of his helmet,
Unable to guard his own goods. It will do no harm to abandon
The stage effects at the shows of Cybele, Flora, and Ceres;
Human comings and goings are really much more amusing!
Is there more fun to be had in watching men bouncing off spring-
   boards,
Sliding down the tightrope, than there is in your own silly antics?
A dweller whose permanent home is a wretched Corycian vessel

Bounced up and down by the waves, by winds from the south and
    the northwest,
A desperate huckster of stuff that stinks and is not too expensive,
You rejoice to import sticky wine from the shores of old Crete,
Flagons and jars and flasks you can say are Jove's fellow townsmen,
Yet the man who plants the soles of his feet on the tightrope
Makes a living from that, and it keeps him from cold and from
    hunger.
You take risks, but for what? A thousand talents of silver,
A hundred country estates. Look at our sea and our harbors
Filled with mighty ships. Most of the population
Now is at sea. A fleet, wherever your hope of a profit
Calls it to sail, will come, beyond Carpathian waters,
Past Gaetulian seas, beyond the straits of Gibraltar,
Westward, to hear the sun hissing in Hercules' ocean.
It is a noble return for all this trouble to sail home
Proud, with purse stretched tight and moneybags full, having wit-
    nessed
Ocean's awful freaks, including her juvenile mermen.

No one madness pursues all men: we think of Orestes
In Electra's arms, facing the fire of the Furies;
Ajax slaughters an ox, and thinks Agamemnon bellows
Or the Ithacan roars. A man is in need of a keeper,
Though he may not be tearing his cloak or his tunic to pieces,
If he loads his ship to the gunwale with goods, and has only
One plank between him and the deep, and the cause of his hardship,
The reason for all this risk, is silver, cut into cartwheels,
Little ones, stamped with minute mottoes and miniature portraits.
Clouds and lightning come up. "Cast off!" cries the owner, whose
    cargo,

Pepper or wheat, fills the hold. "It's nothing really, that color
Of sky, that bundle of black—summer lightning and thunder,
Nothing to it at all!" But this very night the poor fellow
Runs a good chance to be flung overboard as the timbers are broken,
Overwhelmed by the wave, but hanging on to his wallet
With his teeth or left hand. Yesterday not all the gold ore
Tagus carries along, or the red-colored sand of Pactolus
Would have sated his need, but today he is lucky in having
Rags to cover his crotch, and a crust of bread; he's a beggar
Painting pictures of storm, a shipwrecked pleader for pennies.

Property won by such ills is kept with fear and with trouble
Even greater still; it is wretched to guard a huge fortune.
Plutocrat that he is, Licinius orders a cohort
Of his slave boys to stand on guard all night, with fire buckets
Ready at hand; he fears for his amber, his statues, his marble
Brought from Phrygian shores, his ivory, tortoise-shell badges.
Diogenes' barrel won't burn; if it breaks, he can make a new house
On the next day, or patch this with a staple or two and some sol-
    der.
Alexander knew, when he looked at that tub's great dweller,
How much more happy the man who wanted nothing, how wretched
The one who claimed for himself the whole world, willing to suffer
Dangers as great as his deeds. You'd have no divinity, Fortune,
If we had any sense. It is we who have made you a goddess.

Yet, if any one asks me how much is sufficient, I'll tell him:
As much as hunger and thirst and cold are demanding; as much
As sufficed Epicurus, content with his little garden;
As much as the household gods of Socrates had in the old days.
Nature never dictates one thing and Wisdom another.

172

Do I seem to be hemming you in with narrow precedents? Well,
    then,
Copy our customs a bit, take a sum that the emperor Otho
Puts in the first fourteen rows; if you still feel like frowning and
    pouting,
Take a couple of knights, or twelve hundred thousand sesterces!
If I have not even yet filled your lap, if you still are demanding,
Nothing will ever suffice you, neither the riches of Croesus
Nor the Persian realms, nor the fortunes which Claudius Caesar
Gave to Narcissus, whose orders he took when he killed Messalina.

On the atrocities of Egypt

VOLUSIUS, who does not know what monsters lunatic Egypt
Chooses to cherish? One part goes in for crocodile worship;
One bows down to the ibis that feeds upon serpents; elsewhere
A golden effigy shines, of a long-tailed holy monkey!
Where the magic chords resound from Memnon, half-broken,
Where with her hundred gates old Thebes lies buried in ruins,
Whole towns revere a dog, or cats, or a fish from the river.
No one worships Diana. But they have a taboo about biting
Into a leek or an onion; this, they think, is unseemly.
Oh, what holy folk, whose gardens give birth to such gods!
Lamb and the flesh of kid are forbidden to every man's table;
Feeding on human meat, however, is perfectly proper.

When Ulysses told stories like this in Phaeacia,
King Alcinous was more than bemused, and some people
Rose in wrath, and the rest laughed at the vagabond liar.
"Why doesn't somebody throw this tramp in the sea? He deserves
    it—
What he ought to get is his own Charybdis, a real one,
For these lies he makes up, Laestrygonian monsters and Cyclops.
I would sooner believe in the Clashing Rocks or in Scylla,
Or in skins full of storms, or that yarn of the crew and Elpenor
Grunting, changed into pigs at the tap of the light wand of Circe.
What does he think we are—a people utterly brainless?"
That's what a man might say before he was drunk, or had swallowed
More than a sip or two from Phaeacia's powerful wine bowls.
The songs the Ithacan sang had never a witness to prove them.

I have a story to tell, hard to believe, but it happened
Not too long ago, in the year when Juncus was consul.
This took place near the walls of the torrid village of Coptus,
A crime of the crowd, and worse than any the dramatists tell of.
Turn every tragic page, from the era of Pyrrha to our time
And you will never find a crime that a race has committed,
Not till now, so learn of this barbarous innovation.

There are two neighboring towns, Ombi by name, and Tentyra,
Burning with hate for each other, a rivalry deep and long-lasting,
A wound that can never be healed. On each side passionate fury
Rises high, and the people despise the gods of their neighbors,
Thinking that only their own are the kind that deserve recognition.
When it was time for a feast, the leaders and chiefs of one village
Thought it a wonderful chance to interfere with the other,
So that they might not enjoy a day that was happy and festive,

Nor the banquet's delight, on a lavish scale, with the tables
Spread near the temples and crossways, the revels to last a whole
    week,
Couches where nobody sleeps. Egypt is surely uncouth
But when it comes to indulgence (and this I have noted in person),
Its barbarian mobs can compete with Canopus's *haut monde.*
Victory should not be hard when the enemy's half-seas over,
Stammering, staggering drunk. On one side fellows were dancing
While a blackamoor piped; they were all smeared up with their
    unguents,
Wearing flowers for hats, with garlands hiding their foreheads.
On the other side was hate, and the hate was hungry.
They begin to sound with taunting words as a prelude,
These are the trumpet calls to spirits eager for brawling.
Then come replies in kind, ugly and loud, and a clashing
Where the naked fist performs as well as a weapon.
Few are the jaws with no wound, and fewer still are the noses
Unbashed in in the fight. Along the length of the columns
You would see fractions of faces, unrecognizable features,
Bones gaping through broken cheeks, fists that are bloody from
    punching
Enemies in the eye. But still, they think they are fooling,
Playing at war, like kids, because they're not stomping on corpses.
And certainly what is the sense of so many thousands a-brawling
If nobody gets killed? And so the attack becomes fiercer.
Raking the ground with their arms for stones, their natural weapons
For this sort of melee, they begin to lift them, to hurl them—
No such stones, of course, as were thrown by Ajax or Turnus,
No such rock as the one Diomedes flung at Aeneas
Hitting his hip. Right hands, these days, have no such strength in
    them.

Even in Homer's time the race was going to pieces,
And what earth bears now is men who are evil but puny
So that any god who sees them hates them, with laughter!

I've been digressing too long. Let's get back to our story.
Re-enforcements arrived. One side, tremendously heartened,
Dared to draw the sword, to press the battle with arrows.
The Ombites charge, and those who live in the shade of the palm
        trees
Near Tentyra town, retreat in panic confusion.
One of them goes too fast, goes down in his terror, is captured,
Cut into little bits, one dead man in morsels, a banquet
Eaten up, bones and all, by the victorious rabble.
They did not bother to turn him on spits or stew him in kettles.
Building a fire, they thought, was a long and tedious process.
Better gobble him raw.
                        For this, at least, we are grateful
In that the holy fire Prometheus brought down from the heavens
Suffered no taint of pollution. I offer my felicitations
To that element, then, and trust you share my rejoicing.
The man who had the strength to fasten his teeth in a body
Never tasted a thing he enjoyed any more than this meat.
Do not pause to ask whether only the first man who tasted
Sensed, in this horrible act, the satisfactions of pleasure.
After the corpse was consumed, all gone, the last man in the column
Dabbled his hands on the ground, and licked the blood off his
        fingers.

The Vascones, so we are told, prolonged their lives by such measures
Once upon a time. But that was a different story:
Fortune's hatred, war's last threat, extreme desperation,

Long-enduring siege, dire need, a terrible famine,
All added up to acts which ought to arouse us to pity.
After all of the grass, after all of the living creatures,
Everything to which the gnawing of empty bellies
Drove their desperate need, had all been consumed, and their pallor,
Leanness, wasted limbs, drew even their enemies' pity,
Then and only then did they tear, in the fierceness of hunger,
Other men's limbs; indeed, they were ready to feed on their own.
Who of men or of gods would refuse to pardon these starving?
Even their victims' shades would be inclined to forgiveness.
Zeno teaches us better: that Stoic master has shown us
Many things, but not all, should be done for life's preservation.
But how would Spaniards know this, as long ago as Metellus?
Now the whole world has a Greek and Italian Athens;
Gaul with her eloquence has instructed the pleaders of Britain;
Even far-off Thule is talking of hiring professors.
Yet these Vascones I have named were a noble people,
So were the Saguntines, equal in manly devotion,
Worse in the fate they endured, but Egypt is even more savage
Than the altar that waits by the sea of Azov for strangers.
There, if we can believe the stories the poets have left us,
She who founded those rites—unspeakable!—still is contented
With the infliction of death, and the victim need fear nothing fur-
    ther,
Nothing more grim than the knife. But what calamity was it
Drove the Egyptians to crimes like this? What infamous hunger,
What implacable host at their walls could ever have forced them
To this monstrous crime, this utterly loathsome defilement?
What could they do any worse, if the land of Memphis were drying,
Parched with drought, and Nile refused to rise to relieve them?
No wild Cimbrian man, no barbarous Briton, no savage

Horde from the steppes, no monstrous Agathyrsians ever
Raged like this weak mob, this useless and cowardly rabble,
Hoisting their patches of sail on the masts of their crockery vessels,
Pulling their puny oars on painted earthenware dinghies.
A punishment fitting the crime you never will find for these people
In whose minds, it seems, anger is equal to hunger.
Nature, who gave men tears, admits that she gave to them also
Kindly hearts, and these are the source of our noblest feelings.
Nature tells us to weep when a friend is made a defendant,
Downcast, pleading his case; to grieve when a ward, whose com-
    plexion
Might be a boy's or a girl's, summons a swindler to trial.
We sigh at Nature's command, when earth closes over a baby
Too young for the funeral pyre, or the death of a virgin confronts us,
Not her wedding day. What man who is good and deserving,
Worthy the mystic torch, as the priest of Ceres would have him,
Thinks that he has no share in another man's grief and misfortune?
Sympathy makes us distinct from the brutes; so we, of all creatures,
Are the only ones with an inborn sense of compassion,
With a divine potential, an aptitude for expanding
Life's creative arts, having derived from the heavens
Feeling denied those who go on all fours, whose gaze is fixed down-
    ward.
In the first days of the world, our common creator endowed them
Only with life, nothing more, but to us he also gave spirit
So that mutual love would demand our giving and taking
Mutual comfort and aid. The scattered assembled as peoples
Leaving their ancient groves and the woods their ancestors dwelt in,
Building homes for themselves, and for the gods of the household
Adding neighbors next door, making their slumbers more peaceful,
Safe in the trust of men near, their armor affording protection.

If a citizen falls, or staggers, terribly wounded,
Sound the battle call on our common trumpet; common
Be our walls of defence, with one key that locks all of our gateways.

Ah, but today we have a closer agreement of vipers
Than among ourselves; a beast that is marked like another
Acts with more kindness than we; and when did the stronger lion
Take the weaker one's life? In what grove has the wild boar
Ever gone down in death because of a bigger one's tusks?
Indian tigers dwell in peace with Indian tigers,
Bears get along with bears. Only the bloodthirsty human
Thinks it not enough to have forged on impious anvils
Fatal iron and steel. Primitive smiths were accustomed
To beat on their forges the rake, the hoe, the spade, and the plough-
    share,
Tiring themselves at their craft, but they never were makers of sword
    blades.
Now we look upon men whose wrath is not sated by murder:
Killing is not enough; they think they must have for their victuals
A human breast, face, arms. Suppose Pythagoras witnessed
Any such horrors as these? What would he say? To what refuge
Flee in despair? In his creed the beasts of the field were all sacred
Even as man himself, and, more than that, he was careful
Not to stuff his gut with indiscriminate fodder.

On the prerogatives of the soldier

GALLIUS, who can count up the rewards of a term in the army,
Granted moderate luck? If I could go to cantonments
Under a lucky star, let the gate swing open, I'm willing,
Though a trembling recruit. For one hour of a fate that is kindly
Has more value and worth than a letter of recommendation
Sent by Venus to Mars, or a missive sent by his mother,
Juno, who takes delight in the sandy beaches of Samos.

Let us consider first what special advantages soldiers,
All of them, have over everyone else. Not least is the fact that
No civilian dares beat you; what's more, if you give him a beating,
He has to keep his mouth shut, he dare not show to the praetor

Teeth that have been knocked loose, or the gorgeous black and blue
    shiner
You have hung under the eye which the doctor won't promise to
    salvage.
If he takes it to court, the judge he gets is a noncom,
Rough and tough, with hobnailed boots, and a thick-muscled jury,
All in accord with the old camp law and the code of Camillus—
Let no soldier conduct litigation away from the standards.
"In a soldier's case, of course, the centurion's verdict
Is by far the most just, and vengeance will never be lacking
If the suit I bring has the slightest basis of merit."
But the whole cohort is hostile; the maniples, down to a man,
Are in effective agreement to have the redress you are asking
Come out worse than the wrong you complained about in the first
    place.
Since you have two shins, you must have the brains of a jackass,
Such as Vagellius has, that wonderful pleader, to challenge
The envy of so many boots and all those thousands of hobnails.
Who, besides, would be so far from the city, attend you
Like a Pylades, beyond the moat and the rampart?
Better dry our tears, and save our friends from annoyance
Since the most they can do will be to offer excuses.
"Call your witness," the judge will say; but who will be daring,
Bold enough, though he saw the fight, to acknowledge, "I saw it"?
If there is such a man, I consider him worthy of having
Our ancestors' beards and long hair. You can find, much more
    quickly, a witness
Who will perjure himself against a civilian's lawsuit
Than you will get one to tell the truth if it injures the interests
Or the good name of a soldier.

                    Let's look at some other matters,
Perquisites and rewards that go with a term in the army.
If some crook of a neighbor has helped himself to a valley
Or a field of the land my ancestors left, if he's dug up
The sacred boundary stone to which, each year, I give honor
Bringing my wheaten cakes; if a debtor refuses to pay me
Money he's borrowed, and claims that the signature's forged, and
      the papers
Fraudulent, null and void, I shall have to wait for the season
When the whole world goes to court, and the calendar's terribly
      crowded.
Even then there will be delays by the thousands, postponements
Hard to endure. You know how it is: it happens so often.
The benches are all set up, and Caedicius, that eloquent lawyer,
Is putting his cloak aside, when Fuscus departs from the courtroom,
Needing to take a piss: and so, though everything's ready,
Court is adjourned, we depart, resigned to fighting our battles
In that tedious, slow, unyielding sand of the courtroom.
But for those whom their arms protect, whose belts buckle round
      them,
Their own will sets the time to schedule actions against them,
Nor is their substance worn down by the law's long lingering daw-
      dling.

Soldiers alone possess the right of making their wills
While their fathers are living. Payment earned in the service,
So runs the law, is exempt from the sum and substance the father
Has under his control. Therefore Coranus's sire,
Trembling old man that he is, plays up to his son, since the latter
Follows the standards and earns the stipend accorded for service.
Duties well performed reward the son with promotion

Since it would certainly seem to be to the leader's advantage
That his bravest man should be the most prosperous also,
That they should all rejoice in medals and decorations,
That they should all

THE POEM BREAKS OFF AT THIS POINT, IN THE MIDDLE OF A SENTENCE;
SCHOLARS HAVE NO EXPLANATION, BUT SEEM AGREED THAT JUVENAL
PROBABLY INTENDED A POEM OF APPROXIMATELY THREE HUNDRED LINES,
SO THAT SATIRE XVI REALLY IS ONLY ABOUT A QUARTER OF A FULL POEM.